The Humble God

D. Densil Morgan is Professor of Theology and Head of the School of Arts and Humanities at the University of Wales, Bangor. He has written extensively on the history of Christianity and on the Nonconformist tradition. He is a Baptist minister.

THE HUMBLE GOD

A basic course in Christian doctrine

D. Densil Morgan

CANTERBURY
PRESS
Norwich

First published in 2005 by the Canterbury Press Norwich
(a publishing imprint of Hymns Ancient & Modern Limited,
a registered charity)
St Mary's Works, St Mary's Plain,
Norwich, Norfolk, NR3 3BH

www.scm-canterburypress.co.uk

British Library Cataloguing in Publication data

A catalogue record for this book is available
from the British Library

ISBN 1–85311–670–X/9781–85311–670–4

Typeset by Regent Typesetting, London
Printed and bound by
Bookmarque, Croydon, Surrey

Contents

'God is not proud. In his high majesty he is humble.'

Karl Barth, *Church Dogmatics* IV/1, p. 159

Preface

It has been my privilege for the last fifteen years or so to introduce university students to the study and riches of the Christian faith. Six years of pastoral ministry before that were taken up with, among other things, Bible study and pulpit preparation in which the key Christian doctrines were applied to the problems and joys of a village congregation in what was then industrialized South Wales. I have had the pleasure not only of grappling with the truth of the Christian faith and trying better to understand it myself, but of attempting to convey it to numerous audiences, some of whom were students and others lay people who were keen to know more about 'the faith that was once for all entrusted to the saints'. When the invitation came to write the Archbishop of Wales' Lent book, I decided that I would attempt to compose a modest précis of what I have learned and what I have tried to teach over those years.

A brief perusal of the footnotes will show to whom I have been most indebted while preparing this volume. Those who know me will not be surprised by the names listed or by the particular stance that I have taken. The contemporary Princeton theologian George Hunsinger has written winsomely about 'generous orthodoxy'. If this book is recognized as an exercise in such a thing, I will be well pleased.

The invitation to write a Lent book came initially from the previous Archbishop of Wales, the Most Revd Rowan

Williams, and following his move to Lambeth Palace I was most gratified that it was not withdrawn by his successor, the Most Revd Barry Morgan. I would like to register my deep appreciation of their kindness in entrusting the work to a Welsh Nonconformist and a Baptist to boot. During its writing my memory has been drawn back again and again to the incomparable seminars on Christian doctrine under the tutelage of Professor E. Stanley John in the School of Theology at Bangor during 1977–79. My debt to him, as to others of my teachers, is lasting and deep. Christine Smith and the staff of the Canterbury Press have been kindness itself, not only in committing themselves to the book's production but also by the care shown in each part of the publication process.

The questions listed at the end of each chapter are suggested to form a basis for discussion and further reflection. I hope individuals will benefit from reading the book but I have also kept in mind group study, whether among college or university classes, lay training seminars or weeknight meetings of local congregations. As a study of Christian doctrine in the round, the book's focus is beyond that of Lent alone. However, as Christian teaching has the life, death and resurrection of Christ at its heart, Chapters 5–8 could best be suited to reflection during the Church's key season.

D. Densil Morgan
2006

I

To Begin at the Beginning
The Question of Faith

Introduction

In his letter to the Colossian church, the apostle Paul encourages his listeners to root themselves deeply in Christ so that they may be built up sturdily on him. The two metaphors which he uses are those of the root and the foundation: 'As you therefore have received Christ Jesus the Lord, continue to live your lives in him, rooted and built up in him and established in the faith, just as you were taught, abounding in thanksgiving' (Col. 2.6–7). The first metaphor is taken from the world of nature and the second from the human world. By taking in nourishment through the soil, the plant is fed and sustained becoming healthy and strong. A structure or building having been planned and constructed with care can withstand the ravages of climate and circumstance and remain not only a monument to the architect's craft but a fitting dwelling as well. Scripture constantly uses both these metaphors in order to emphasize not only the dynamic character of Christian faith, that it is dependent on a living relationship with God in Christ through the Spirit, but also the fact that we, too, are called to build carefully and ensure that we stand and not fall (John 15.1–16; Matt. 7.24–8). And all is to be done 'in thanksgiving'. It was the great Swiss theologian Karl Barth who wrote – many times – that the only fitting response to grace (*charis*) is thanksgiving (*eucharistia*).[1] This modest study of Christian doctrine, or teaching, will strive to keep this point in mind throughout.

What follows is a short exposition of some of the basic teachings of the Christian church. It is by no stretch of the imagination exhaustive, neither does it purport to be original. It is, rather, a précis of some of the cardinal doctrines of our faith written in the conviction that not only do they 'make sense' in themselves, and of the world in which we live, but that they are true. No attempt will be made to 'prove' the truth of the Christian contention on the basis of some reality outside of the Christian faith itself. Such an undertaking would be ill conceived at best and misleading; it would imply that Christianity needs some external support and that it can not be rationally affirmed unless it has passed the test of an alien logic. A building like that would be rickety in the extreme! The Christian realities shine in their own light and the church's claim that the eternal God both exists – 'I am who I am' (Exod. 3.14) – and has graciously turned towards humankind in Jesus Christ is not something which has been deduced from some innate religious premise or according to natural human insight, but is the result of God's self-revelation in scripture. This revelation possesses its own logic and rationale which, although not in opposition to unbaptized human reason, challenges it radically at crucial points. Human reason, like everything else, functions best in its own sphere: in order to operate properly in the realm of our knowledge of God, it must be judged, justified, redeemed and set free by the gospel of Christ.

In order for the Christian claims to make sense, our attitude must be one of trust, obedience and humility and a sincere desire to understand.

---

1 E.g. Karl Barth, *Church Dogmatics* IV/1, *The Doctrine of Reconciliation* (Edinburgh: T & T Clark, 1956), p. 41.

No one is likely to make much of Christian theology
unless he has some awareness of what worship, prayer,
the sense of sin, moral constraint, atonement, forgiveness, gratitude, love, and obedience signify, and unless
he has some imaginative understanding of the peculiar
nature of the compulsion exercised by the figure of Jesus
Christ.[2]

Although written well over a generation ago – and predat-
ing the advent of inclusive language – the wisdom of those
words remains. There is only one way to do justice to the
task at hand, by having an approach which is willing to
affirm the reality of the Christian claims if convinced that
they are true. So before we embark on a study of the different doctrines of the Christian faith – God as Creator and
Trinity, the person and work of Christ, humankind, the
Holy Spirit and the like – we need to say something about
our basic attitude to the work, and then something about
the basis upon which we make our assertions. In other
words, we will begin by considering the concept of faith,
and then discuss the idea of revelation.

The Role of Faith

Faith means trust and trust, whether it be trust in God
or humanity or history or the world around, is essential
for human existence. We need a measure of confidence in
our circumstances, a sense of the reliability of those things
with which we must deal and of the people with whom we
have to do. Trust, therefore, depends upon circumstances
or things or people. This, according to Wolfhart Pannenberg, is 'the basic condition for the formation of a healthy

---

2 Daniel T. Jenkins, *The Scope of Theology* (New York: The World
Publishing Company, 1965), p. x.

personality'.[3] Such trust, usually, can be taken for granted. In normal circumstances we are quite unconscious of the basis for our trust. It is only when that basis is threatened or collapses that we realize the nature of our trust and how dependent upon it we really are.

The biblical revelation makes it clear that the primary object of Christian trust is God, Yahweh, the Lord, the Creator-Redeemer God who was first revealed in the Old Testament scriptures and supremely in the New Testament Christ. As creator and redeemer God's claim upon his people is total. Their response in obedience and faith should be similarly unconditional. The biblical polemic against idolatry, the literal worship of inanimate objects in the Old Testament (Isa. 40.18–25; 44.1–20; 46.1–2; cf. Exod. 20.3–4) and the giving of priority to interests other than God in the New Testament (Eph. 5.5; Phil. 3.19; Col. 3.5), emphasizes the danger of misplaced trust. By choosing to trust the idol, which is some aspect of the created order, rather than the creator, individuals display an inauthentic loyalty which demands the same degree of obligation as that demanded by God. As both lay claim to an individual's supreme devotion there can be no question of peaceful co-existence between them. So men and women are put in the position of having to choose. Obedience to God's demand implies repentance and faith and leads to conversion and a commitment which, according to the Christian estimate, is authentic. Thus faith finds its goal and fulfilment in its true object, which is God.

This faith is both a human decision and a divine gift. The act of faith is indubitably my act. It is I who choose to forsake myself, to believe in God and to trust in Christ (Mark 8.34; Matt. 11.28–29). However, I do so solely in response to the prior initiative of a gracious God. My faith, though

---

3 Wolfhart Pannenberg, *The Apostles' Creed in the Light of Today's Questions* (London: SCM Press, 1972), p. 4.

wholly my own, is made possible only in the freedom of God's grace (cf. Eph. 2.8). This emphasis, which is faithful to the conviction that salvation is of *God*, is essential to prevent faith from becoming a 'work', a human activity independent of God, which leads to self-justification. Faith, then, must never be confused with subjective religious feelings, attitudes or emotions, or factual theological knowledge even if correct, orthodox and sound, *my* feelings about God's love towards me or *my* knowledge of the scriptures or the gospel or the like: 'Let the one who boasts, boast in the Lord!' (1 Cor. 1. 31). On the contrary, faith must find its justification from outside of itself, from its object, from that on which it relies.

> Our salvation is external to ourselves. I find no salvation in my life history, but only in the history of Jesus Christ. Only the one who allows himself to be found in Jesus Christ, in his incarnation, his cross and his resurrection, is with God and God with him.[4]

Finding its objective counterpoint in God, the living and gracious God who has been revealed in Jesus Christ, faith is free to develop, to change, constantly to be redefined and hopefully perfected in the flux of new situations and broadening horizons. Its validity, veracity and continuity are guaranteed not by any inherent virtue – individuals' faith can often be pathetically weak, fractured and unstable – but by the continuing promise of the gracious God. Within the relationship of faith everything depends upon the reliability of the one in whom we trust. The basis for that trust, according to the church's conviction, is Jesus Christ. It is in him, who is before all things and in whom all things hold together, that God has pledged his faithfulness to

---

4 Dietrich Bonhoeffer, *Life Together: Dietrich Bonhoeffer Works*, vol. 5 (Minneapolis: Fortress Press, 1996), p.62.

humankind: 'For in him all the fullness of God was pleased to dwell, and through him God was pleased to reconcile to himself all things, whether on earth or in heaven, by making peace through the blood of his cross' (Col. 1.19–20).

Faith, therefore, is multifaceted. It is both trust and commitment, human and divine. It implies knowledge and assent as well as an absolute dependence upon the person on whom it relies, in this case God in Jesus Christ. Although the element of dependence is paramount it is not a blind dependence, a vacuous attitude of confidence in an unknown or unknowable 'God'. Rather it is a process of trust and commitment involving head, heart and will on the basis of reasonable evidence. That evidence is posited to us in the scriptures, the history of Israel as the people of God in the Old Testament and the story of Jesus Christ, his birth, life, death and resurrection in the New Testament, along with the history and development of the Christian community, the Body of Christ, in the world. We will have more to say about the scriptures, God's Word, in the next chapter. Suffice it to note here that the evidence for God's existence and acts in the Bible is sound and should readily commend the Christian's assent. And faith, dependent as it is on its object, is profoundly rational. 'Christian faith is not irrational, not anti-rational, not supra-rational, but rational in its proper sense.'[5] Rationality, in this sense, is not a free-standing enterprise, an autonomous entity and a rule unto itself but it is tethered to its object; it is the logical and considered response of the intellect to its God. Just as God exists antecedently as Father, Son and Holy Spirit and has defined himself as the One who has turned to humankind in grace, faith is the creaturely affirmation of this fact. Not for nothing has Christian theology spoken of the rationality of faith and its relation to the divine Logos

---

5 Karl Barth, *Dogmatics in Outline* (London: SCM Press, 1958), p. 23.

or Word. 'Christian faith and knowledge of Christian faith takes place at the point where the divine reason, the divine Logos, sets up his law in the region of man's understanding, to which law human, creaturely reason must accommodate itself.'[6] It is cool and reasonable and functions in the realm of time, history and fact:

> We declare to you what was from the beginning, what we have *heard*, what we have *seen with our eyes*, what we have *looked at and touched with our hands*, concerning the word of life – this life was revealed, and we have seen it and testify to it, and declare to you the eternal life that was with the Father and was revealed to us – we declare to you what we have seen and heard so that you also may have fellowship with us; and truly our fellowship is with the Father and with his Son Jesus Christ. (1 John 1.1–3)

Faith, set free by the Spirit, affirms the objective, time-bound, factual reality of God's specific involvement with human beings in Christ. It is not a matter of 'believing what we know is not true'(!) or an irrational 'leap into the dark' or venturing forth on flimsy evidence or on no evidence at all. 'To trust God is *not* taking a chance, leaping into darkness, or gambling or betting,'[7] but a considered response to compelling evidence, the validity of which impinges itself upon us in the light of God's self-revelation in the gospel. So whereas faith is not merely an intellectual assent to facts and propositions, the propositions are nevertheless important. Believing them to be reliable, a person is in a position to forsake him- or herself and cleave to the person who embodies the propositions or to whom the facts witness.

---

6 Barth, *Dogmatics in Outline*, p. 24.
7 Karl Barth, *The Faith of the Church: A Commentary on the Apostles' Creed* (London: Fontana Books, 1960), p. 39.

He or she can now be committed, in absolute dependence, to the gracious God in Christ.

The Object of Faith

The object of faith, according to this claim, is God, the biblical Lord and Father of the saviour Jesus Christ. Such an exact definition can be made on the basis of the biblical narrative itself. There is, however, ample evidence from the scriptures that some measure of divine knowledge can be gleaned from natural sources, from the external world and from the internal witness of the human conscience, in other words from reason and from morality. The apostle Paul in Romans 1 presupposes the fact that there exists a definite and incontestable revelation of God in creation:

> For what can be known about God is plain ... because God has shown it ... Ever since the creation of the world his eternal power and divine nature, invisible though they are, have been understood and seen through the things he has made. (Rom. 1.19–20)

In other words, humans possess not so much an innate, intuitive, positive and instinctive feeling for the divine but an objective knowledge of God gleaned from his works. Yet the status of this knowledge, as we shall see, is highly problematical. Rather than leading people to God, what it does, it seems, is to condemn them! 'For though they knew God, they did not honour him as God or give thanks to him, but they became futile in their thinking, and their senseless minds were darkened' (Rom. 1.21). That is why, in his address to the Athenian philosophers in the Book of Acts, Paul claims that something new, innovative and altogether revolutionary is needed in order to overcome people's disregard for and perversion of this objective revelation in nature: 'What therefore you worship as unknown, this I proclaim to you' (Acts 17.23). So despite the fact of natural revelation, it only possesses limited usefulness in the search for a satisfying and truthful knowledge of God.

In the course of Christian history many theologians have echoed this same conviction. The Protestant Reformer John Calvin (1509–64), for instance, waxed eloquent on the subject of the *sensum divinitatis* in the human conscience, that is, individuals' universal awareness of the reality of God: 'To prevent anyone from taking refuge in the pretence of ignorance, God himself has implanted in all men a certain understanding of his divine majesty.'[8] Yet Calvin was equally insistent that this sense of God had been impaired and nullified by the corruption of sin. The *semen religionis*, 'the seed of religion sown in all people', will never develop into a correct, wholesome and sound knowledge of God, he claimed. 'Scarcely one in a hundred is met who fosters it, once received, in the heart, and none in whom it ripens, much less shows fruit in season.'[9] According to this conviction, God's natural or general revelation of himself in creation and conscience are repressed; in order to yield a valid and wholesome knowledge of God, the sense of God's presence gleaned by general revelation needs to be released, clarified and corrected in the light of something else.

Because of this insufficiency, natural revelation needs to be authenticated and endorsed by a more particular revelation of God. The conviction which will govern this study is that particular revelation is to be found in the person of Jesus Christ as witnessed to in scripture. The locus of revelation will be the historical Christ and the documents, both Old Testament and New, deemed authoritative by the church as witnessing to him. In Christ, God has revealed

---

8 John Calvin, *Institutes of the Christian Religion* 1.3.1 (Philadelphia: Westminster Press, 1960), p. 43.
9 Calvin, *Institutes*, p. 47.

himself clearly and definitively having turned towards humankind, and the Bible, the Old Testament as preparation and the New Testament as fulfilment, is a truthful and dependable record of this self-disclosure. 'Long ago God spoke to our ancestors in many and various ways by the prophets, but in these last days he has spoken to us by a Son' (Heb. 1.1). The theological significance of the Bible is that it witnesses to God's activity in the Word and that Word is Christ: 'In the beginning was the Word, and the Word was with God, and the Word was God ... And the Word became flesh and lived among us, and we have seen his glory as of the Father's only Son, full of grace and truth' (John 1.1, 14). The preparation for Christ in the Old Testament, his life, death and resurrection in the New, partake of the character of revelation, revealing to us what we need to know about God, his nature, power and very being. Without this particular revelation in Christ, which assures us of God's grace and loving kindness towards us, we would know nothing of any substance and assurance about God. However this conviction is to be formulated in a pluralistic, religiously diverse postmodern culture, it will remain the touchstone for our understanding of our task.

The fact that Christians claim that the self-revelation of God has occurred finally and definitively in Christ has never meant the resolution of all questions or the clarification of all mysteries. Revelation remains a revelation of *God*, and God, despite the coming of Christ, is not directly perceptible. 'No one has ever seen God', says the Gospel of John (John 1.18); 'God is spirit', said Jesus to the Samarian woman at the well, 'and those who worship him must worship in spirit and truth' (John 4.24). Even within the context of its underlying clarity, revelation will always retain an element of elusiveness and ambiguity. God can never be domesticated or possessed or (by us) fully understood. The New Testament gospel is regularly referred to as a mystery

(1 Cor. 2.7; 4.1; Col. 2.2; Eph. 1.9), that is, it is not self-evident or readily understood. The apostle Paul becomes positively lyrical when contemplating the ineffable character of God's gracious revelation in Christ: 'O the depth of the riches and wisdom and knowledge of God! How unsearchable are his judgements and how inscrutable his ways! "For who has known the mind of the Lord?"' (Rom. 11.33–34). Even when revealed God remains, paradoxically, hidden. He does not reveal the fullness of his being. The revelation conceals more than it actually discloses: 'Truly, you are a God who hides himself, O God of Israel, the Saviour' (Isa. 45.15). The biblical God is always unfathomable even when disclosed: 'As the heavens are higher than the earth, so are my ways higher than your ways and my thoughts than your thoughts' (Isa. 55.9).

Our consideration of Christian faith, therefore, can never lead us to conclude that we have dispatched all the problems or discovered all the answers. The elusive element in revelation will always condition the extent of our theological understanding. 'Evangelical theology is *modest* theology,' says Karl Barth once more, 'because it is determined to be so by its object.'[10] And that object is God.

Questions for Discussion

1 Attempt your own definition of faith.

2 What is the difference between trusting in human beings and trusting in God? Are they connected with one another, or are they mutually exclusive?

3 What does it mean to say that our trust can be misplaced?

10 Karl Barth, *Evangelical Theology: An Introduction* (London: Weidenfeld & Nicolson, 1963), p. 13.

4 What is wrong with the assertion that 'faith is believing in something for which there is no evidence'?

5 Do we possess an innate or natural knowledge of God?

6 How much of God can we know and how much is hidden from us?

2

The Word at Work
The Question of Revelation

The Process of Revelation

It is the conviction of the church that its God is a living God, one who acts in grace and communicates himself: a God who speaks. 'God's action is not speechless, a silent force, an opaque causal power; it has as one of its goals the shedding abroad of the knowledge of itself, and so it speaks.'[1] Through God's revelation God speaks a word to humankind. It is the Bible that witnesses to that revelation and becomes, in its own way, a part of God's disclosure or revelation of himself.

God's disclosure has been preserved in scripture. The unity of holy scripture including the 39 books of the Old Testament canon as well as the 27 which were eventually accepted by the church as constituting the New, is the witness contained therein to Christ and his work from the creation of the world to the consummation of all things by him. It is within the parameters of this unity that the Christian believer, and theologian, will understand his or her faith. The word 'Bible' is of fairly recent origin. It is a medieval misreading of the plural Greek noun *bibliou* = 'books', which became a Latin singular *biblia*. The word

---

1 John Webster, *Word and Church: Essays in Christian Dogmatics* (Edinburgh: T & T Clark, 2001), p. 66.

for scripture, however, goes back to the New Testament it-self. It is derived from the Latin *scriptura* which was used in turn to translate the Greek *graphē* (*graphoi*) = 'writing' (pl. 'writings'), a reference to the Old Testament either in part or in its entirety. These writings recorded the events and the interpretations of these events as well as the rules and rituals that embodied God's self-disclosure to his people.

The process of God's revelation is three-tiered. The first tier can be described as primary or formative revelation, which included that 'series of events set within the plane of human life and historical sequence through which God has specially revealed himself'.[2] This primary revelation was multifaceted. It included, from the Old Testament, such things as personal communication, like that which occurred between God and the patriarchs and the proph-ets, for instance, 'But the Lord said to me ...' (Jer. 1.7); the sort of experience and reflection believed by the church to be divinely inspired, which would become the basis for the psalms and the wisdom literature; historical events like the Exodus from Egypt; and verbal proclamation as when the words of the prophets became God's revelation for that first generation of hearers. This level of revelation was definitive: in it God defined his own nature and require-ments in obedience and worship to the founders or initial recipients of revelation; and would become normative for the subsequent history of the community. Primary or form-ative revelation culminated in the New Testament with the coming of Christ, his incarnation, atonement, resurrection and ascension; thereafter with the experience of the church at Pentecost and after; and finally with the apostolic tes-timony to Christ evidenced by the letters of Paul, Peter, John and the author to the Hebrews. Holy scripture, there-

2 James Barr, 'Revelation through history in the Old Testament and modern theology', in Martin E. Marty and Dean G. Peerman (eds), *New Theology* (New York: The Macmillan Company, 1964), p. 69.

fore, bears witness to that primary and definitive revelation granted by God over thousands of years to the successive first recipients of his Word.

The second stage of revelation involved the production and preservation of a record of these normative events and experiences along with their interpretation in the context of the community's life and faith. It was this record – the pre-history of which is enormously complex – that was eventually accepted by the church as being its authoritative 'canon' or rule of faith. The Old Testament canon, which was finally decided upon as late as the first century BC, became normative for the Christian church due to Christ and his apostles having subjected themselves to its authority. The New Testament canon was finalized in AD 367 when the early church father Athanasius, Bishop of Alexandria in Egypt, circulated his thirty-ninth annual Easter letter to his flock listing the 27 books from Matthew to Revelation as being the final rule and norm for Christian faith and practice. The deciding factor as to which books should be accepted or rejected by the Christian community was their perceived apostolic authorship or authentication, and that their doctrinal content was faithful to Christ's teaching. So the second stage of revelation had to do with the actual text of the Bible which we have inherited according to the tradition of the church.

If the first stage in the process can be described as primary or formative revelation, and the second stage as canonical or secondary revelation, the third and final phase can be termed existential or experiential revelation, that is, when the content of revelation is understood, appropriated and acted upon by the believer within the ongoing life of the church. Thus God's initial revelation made thousands of years ago and mediated to us by way of the scriptures as secondary or canonical revelation becomes immediate and contemporaneous to individuals in their current situation.

This is, in Karl Barth's phrase, 'the event in which the word of man proves itself the Word of God'.

> As to when, where and how the Bible shows itself to us as this event as the Word of God, we do not decide, but the Word of God himself decides, at different times in the church and with different people confirming and renewing the event of instituting and inspiring the prophets and apostles to be his witnesses and servants, so that in their written word they again live before us, not only as those who once spoke in Jerusalem and Samaria, to the Romans and Corinthians, but as those who in all the concretness of their own situation and action speak to us here and now.[3]

Without the illumination of the Holy Spirit at work in us and upon us in sovereign and gracious freedom, revelation can never become personal, God's revelation 'to us here and now'. The objective revelation granted to the fathers, prophets and apostles and faithfully preserved in holy scripture must become subjective – not in any autonomous way but according to the dynamic of God's active relation with his people – or appropriated revelation for ourselves.

The Notion of Inspiration

The Christian church has believed and taught that the Holy Spirit was and is involved in the three phases of revelation. Not only does the Spirit enlighten the mind, enabling it to respond, and release the will, enabling it to obey God's revelation in scripture, but the Spirit was at work in the long and complicated process that lay behind the formation and

---

3 Karl Barth, *Church Dogmatics* I/2, *The Doctrine of the Word of God* (Edinburgh: T & T Clark, 1956), pp. 530–1, translation revised.

transmission of the text. The concept employed traditionally to describe the way in which God's self-disclosure in the scriptures was recorded and preserved is inspiration. The key passage for the church's doctrine of inspiration is 2 Timothy 3.16: 'All scripture is inspired by God and profitable for teaching, reproof, correction and training in righteousness.' The word 'inspired' literally means 'God-breathed' – *theopneustos* – and the idea is that whatever human or mundane methods were used in the formation and transmission of holy scripture, its ultimate source and author is God.

This was believed to be the case in both testaments. In the Old Testament the words of both law and prophets are frequently referred to as the very words of God (1 Kings 22.8–16; Neh. 8; Ps. 119). The Old Testament prophecies were written by those whom the Spirit had moved and guided: 'No prophecy ever came by human will, but men and women moved by the Holy Spirit spoke from God' (2 Pet. 1.21). Christ and the apostles often quote Old Testament texts that equate the words of specific characters with the words of God himself, for example Isaiah (Mark 7.6–8), David (Mark 12.36), while mention of the human author is sometimes dispensed with totally in preference for the divine author behind the human hand, for instance Hebrews 1.5–13.

With the dawning of a new dispensation a new situation arose. Yet as the church began almost immediately to accept the Pauline Epistles as authoritative writings on a par with the Old Testament, the same reasoning which had governed the acceptance of the Old Testament as inspired scripture was now applied to the New. The apostle Paul, for instance, by teaching in Christ's name (2 Thess. 3.6), claiming apostolic authority (1 Cor. 14.37), and by maintaining that the doctrine had been revealed to him by the Spirit (1 Cor. 2.9–13), provided the most definite example of the way in which the writings of the new dispensation should be recognized as the word of God. Christ's own instructions concerning the subsequent apostolic witness to himself recorded in the Gospel of John (14.26; 15.26–7; 16.13–15) also provided the church with guidelines as to how it should recognize future scriptures as God's Word.

This being the case, it is legitimate to claim that the word of scripture should be equated with the very Word of God. As the early church father, Augustine, Bishop of Hippo in North Africa, says in his famous *Confessions*, on God's behalf as it were: 'O man, what my scripture says, I say.'[4] This is not a matter of literalism, or a crude concept of divine dictation. But because 'inspiration ... involves *words*', and 'what revelation impels is writing',[5] the verbal dimension of the Bible cannot be minimized or collapsed into a concept of the author's subjective religious impulses or of the reader's or the listener's spiritual receptiveness. Rather, what inspiration does is to preserve *in writing* God's particuar revelation through a historical and cultural process which did not undercut imperfect and creaturely realities but took them up into itself. Inspiration, therefore, 'simply indicates the inclusion of texts in the sanctifying work of the Spirit so that they may become fitting vessels of the treasure of the gospel'.[6]

The obvious implication to be drawn from the church's doctrine of inspiration is that the words of scripture, which convey divine revelation, are substantially trustworthy. The basic reliability of scripture should never be questioned. The Bible emphasizes repeatedly, in a quite unselfconscious way, that its revelation is to be trusted. The

---

4 St Augustine, *Confessions* XII 44 (Oxford: Oxford University Press, 1991), p. 300.
5 John Webster, *Holy Scripture: A Dogmatic Sketch* (Cambridge: Cambridge University Press, 2003), p. 38.
6 Webster, *Holy Scripture*, p. 39.

prophetic message is *sure*: 'You will do well to be attentive to this as to a lamp shining in a dark place' (2 Pet. 1.19). The word which Paul is charged to commit to Timothy is *trustworthy*, worthy of full acceptance (1 Tim. 1.15; 3.1; 4.9; 2 Tim. 2.11; Titus 3.8). The author of the Letter to the Hebrews makes it plain that salvation, having first been declared by God, has been *attested* – that is, made sure – to us by those who heard him (Heb. 2.3). If men and women are like the withering grass, the Word of God will abide for ever 'and that word is the good news which was preached to you' (1 Pet. 1.24–25). Scripture, gospel and Word are all of a piece. The witness of scripture to itself, consented to by the confession of the church, is that holy scripture is reliable, trustworthy and sure, possessing connotations of authority, certainty and irrefutability. Holy scripture is, in fact, 'God's Word written'.

The Validity of Criticism

A study of the actual text of the Bible, and an appreciation of the complex way in which the Bible developed, will easily convince us that its reliability as revelation does not undermine its human character. While preserving its trustworthy nature, divine inspiration did not obliterate human weaknesses. 'Inspiration does not mean deification ... Inspiration consists in this, that God makes the words of men the instruments of his word, that he uses human words for divine purposes.'[7] The Bible, while retaining its authoritative character as God's Word, is yet a human composition. The Word is revealed to us in the words of *people*: '*Men and women* moved by the Holy Spirit spoke from God' (2 Pet. 1.21). As the contemporary theologian John Webster says:

---

7 Herman Ridderbos, *Studies in Scripture and its Interpretation* (Grand Rapids: Eerdmans, 1978), p. 25.

'Encountering the text of Scripture is encountering a human word which is caught up into revelation, though in such a way that it does not surrender its humanity.'[8] Like Christ, scripture has 'gone into the creaturely, into humanity, weak, despised and ignoble. The Word became writing and has, as writing, subjected itself to the fate of all writing.'[9] The human element in scripture should not be disparaged in the desire to safeguard the Bible as divine revelation.

It is this human element in scripture which includes such phenomena as factual divergences in history and chronology, inaccuracies in reporting and quotation, a seemingly deliberate imprecision in the composition of the narrative complemented by the particular interpretation of the community within which the narrative evolved, as well as the creative contribution of the editors of the text. It also extends to the use of different literary styles, devices and genres such as creation stories, saga, allegory, hyperbole, pseudonymity (the use of a biblical author's name by someone else to claim that person's authority) and the like. For instance, the same events recorded in the books of Kings and Chronicles and in 1 and 2 Samuel are very difficult to reconcile: who actually killed Goliath, was it David or Elhanan? (1 Sam. 17; 2 Sam. 21.19). Then there are factual discrepancies between the different Gospels and examples of inaccurate quotation: according to Matthew Jairus' daughter had just died when Jesus was called upon whereas Mark's account states that she was merely ill when Jesus appeared (Matt. 9.18; Mark 5.22–23). Mark's Gospel begins with the words:

As it is written in the prophet Isaiah,
  'See, I am sending my messenger ahead of you,

---

8 Webster, *Word and Church*, p. 96.
9 Herman Bavinck, *Gereformeerde Dogmatiek*, vol. 1 (Kampen: J. H. Kok, 1976), p. 405.

who will prepare your way;
the voice of one crying out in the wilderness:
"Prepare the way of the Lord ..."' (Mark 1.2–3)

In fact the quotation does not derive from Isaiah at all but from Malachi 3.1 and Exodus 23.30. There is also obvious editorial creativity. The temple-cleaning incident, for example, which John placed at the beginning of his Gospel and at the outset of Jesus' ministry, and the synoptic Gospels place at the very end (John 2.13–17; Matt. 21.12–13; Mark 11.15–17; Luke 19.45–46) indicates how the different evangelists reconstructed the actual historical circumstances which the incident portrays for some dramatic or theological effect. It is patent that the biblical writers are not working with a tight, modern (if, by now, rather dated) concept of factual and historical accuracy which does not undermine scripture's reliability as God's Word but illustrates its nature as a *human* construct: 'It is arguable that the Bible does contain errors and contradictions by modern standards but which are not in fact contrary to its own standards and purposes.'[10] What is essential is that we allow the Bible to control our ideas of the nature of its own composition and not force the Bible into a preconceived scheme of our own.

The same is true in regards to the different literary styles and conventions that the biblical authors employed. We should not expect to find literal truth when the genre used by the authors may be allegorical or mythological. We shall search in vain for the Bible to shed light on matters of science or biology or geology or the like when the biblical authors, who belonged to a pre-scientific culture, had not intended making scientific or biological or geological points. The literary styles of the Bible should be duly

10 I. Howard Marshall, *The Inspiration of Scripture* (London: Hodder & Stoughton, 1982), p. 71.

respected and the integrity of scripture as revelation will not suffer as a result. It is the fact of creatureliness that legitimizes the task of criticism. Textual criticism, historical criticism, redaction and form criticism and the like must be employed not to relativize the Bible's divine content but to shed light on the way in which the text has evolved. What will remain is the text, and it is that, as a living word, that will do what it has always done: lead men and women to Christ and the salvation that he offers: 'You have known the sacred writings that are able to instruct you for salvation through faith in Jesus Christ' (2 Tim. 3.15).

Questions for Discussion

1 Describe the three phases of revelation. In your view is any one more important than the other?

2 How does the Holy Spirit assist us in understanding the Bible?

3 Are there any parts of the Bible that you feel uncomfortable with? If so, how should we think of it as being the Word of God?

4 Are there other religious (or secular) texts that you feel are 'inspired' by God? If so, in which way is the inspiration of the Bible unique?

5 How should we respond to the notion of biblical 'criticism'? Should we criticize the Bible, if it has been inspired by God?

6 Discuss the implications of the verse: 'You search the scriptures because you think that in them you have eternal life; and it is they that testify to me' (John 5.39).

3

The Christian Doctrine of God
The Father Almighty

The Old Testament Evidence

We begin our exploration of Christian theology proper
with the concept of God: who God is and what it is that
we can say about him. As always, we will attempt to do so
in the light of the biblical evidence. The doctrinal significance of the Bible, as we have claimed, is that it witnesses
to and becomes, in its own way, a part of God's disclosure
or revelation of himself. The preliminary revelation was
given to Israel, and it is Yahweh, the Lord of Israel, who
discloses himself ultimately in Jesus Christ, the risen Lord.
This, of course, is a Christian contention, and one which
is axiomatic for the church. The contemporary American
theologian Robert Jenson writes:

> We will follow the one biblical narrative to identify the
> one biblical God, only as we read the Bible by the pur-
> pose by which the church assembled this book in the
> first place, to be in its entirety and all its parts witness to
> Jesus' resurrection and so to a particular God.[1]

It is this story which constitutes the biblical narrative and it
is this continued revelation which forms the unity of both
testaments within the Christian Bible.

---

1 Robert W. Jenson, *Systematic Theology* vol. 1, *The Triune God* (New
York: Oxford University Press, 1997), p. 58.

The most obvious characteristics of God in the Old Testament narrative are those of personhood and transcendence. All God's different attributes – might, power and glory; grace, love, faithfulness and the rest – are shown to be the *personal* attributes of a *transcendent* God. One key passage which illustrates this is to be found towards the beginning of the Book of Exodus:

> Moses was keeping the flock of his father-in-law Jethro, the priest of Midian; he led his flock beyond the wilderness, and came to Horeb, the mountain of God. There the angel of the LORD appeared to him in a flame of fire out of a bush; he looked, and the bush was blazing, yet it was not consumed. Then Moses said, 'I must turn aside and look at this great sight, and see why the bush is not burned up.' When the LORD saw that he had turned aside to see, God called to him out of the bush, 'Moses, Moses!' And he said, 'Here I am.' (Exod. 3.1–4)

God here is more than an influence, an impersonal power: God possesses personhood. God observes Moses, acts in response to Moses's curiosity, God addresses Moses and will soon call him, as representative of his people, into a reciprocal and covenanted relationship with himself. Although God makes this disclosure through the elements of nature, through the flame in the bush, the author of the story is very careful to maintain that God and nature are not one. God is not an aspect of his own creation; God is no idol. Indeed, the absolute nature of the divine character and the finality of God's claims are emphasized to Moses later on in the story, when he is addressed by God on Mount Sinai:

> You shall have no other gods before me. You shall not make for yourself an idol, whether in the form of any-

thing that is in heaven above, or that is on the earth beneath, or that is in the water under the earth. You shall not bow down to them or worship them; for I the LORD your God am a jealous God. (Exod. 20.3–5)

This God cannot be trapped within the confines of creation. He is God, the Lord, the exclusive or particular God, and as such possesses otherness and exists apart from everything else. This otherness is mysterious and unnerving. The fire, although alight, did not exhaust itself; the bush burned but was not consumed:

Then he said, 'Come no closer! Remove the sandals from your feet, for the place on which you are standing is holy ground.' He said further, 'I am the God of your father, the God of Abraham, the God of Isaac, and the God of Jacob.' And Moses hid his face, for he was afraid to look at God. (Exod. 3.5–7)

God, then, is revealed here as both personal being – 'I am the God of Abraham, the God of Isaac, and the God of Jacob' – and as holy, transcendent and numinous being: 'Come no closer ... for the place on which you are standing is holy ground.' Because God is personal, the one who calls Moses by name and identifies himself by naming Moses' forebears and indeed, when asked my Moses to do so, *names himself* as Jahweh, 'I AM WHO I AM' (Exod. 3.14), his transcendence, even if it is unnerving, is never an abstraction: 'Bearing this name, God is not simply holy mystery, the nameless and voiceless whence of some sense of the numinous, an ineffable and indefinite deity.'[2] Rather, God is person: 'I am the LORD, that is my name' (Isa. 42.8),

2 John Webster, *Holiness* (London: SCM Press, 2003), p. 36.

whose intentions reflect his innermost nature and reveal who he *is*:

> Then the LORD said, 'I have observed the misery of my people who are in Egypt; I have heard their cry on account of their taskmasters. Indeed, I know their sufferings, and I have come down to deliver them from the Egyptians, and to bring them up out of that land to a good and broad land, a land flowing with milk and honey. (Exod. 3.7–8)

This God is a loving God who chooses to care for his people, who deigns to respond to their needs and who promises, by his might, to release them from the thraldom of their enemies. God does this because he is *God*, *this* God, the God who has revealed himself as the Holy One of Israel. His holiness is not something which exists apart from his mercy and his intention to dwell among humankind but is, in fact, a reflection of it: 'God's holy majesty, even in its unapproachableness, is not characterized by a sanctity which is abstract difference or otherness, a counter-reality to the profane; it is majesty known in turning, enacted and manifest in the works of God.'[3] In other words, God is the one who turns towards his people in mercy, salvation and redemption, instituting a relationship with them which will never be broken. All this is implicit in God's personhood *and* his transcendence, both of which, according to the biblical story, are aspects of who God is:

> God's holiness is his otherness, his sheer difference from everything else. It expresses itself negatively in a rejection of all that is unworthy to come into his presence, more positively in his establishing of the goodness of the creature that is other than he.[4]

---

3 Webster, *Holiness*, p. 41.
4 Colin E. Gunton, The *Christian Faith: An Introduction to Christian Doctrine* (Oxford: Blackwell, 2002), p. 49.

Such is the thrust not only of this striking passage in the beginning of the Book of Exodus but of the whole Bible in its depiction of God.

Although it is not a central Old Testament motif, these attributes of loving, caring strength are emphasized by the metaphor of fatherhood. God's love within the covenant is a parental love. Challenging Pharaoh through the words of Moses, God says: 'Israel is my firstborn son. I said to you, "Let my son go that he may worship me"'(Exod. 4.22–23). Neither is this figure confined to the Exodus narrative. It is reiterated by the prophets and in the Book of Psalms:

> For you are our father,
>   though Abraham does not know us and Israel does
>   not acknowledge us;
> you, O LORD, are our father;
> our Redeemer from of old is your name. (Isa. 63.16)

> Is Ephraim my dear son?
>   Is he the child I delight in?
> As often as I speak against him,
>   I still remember him.
> Therefore I am deeply moved for him;
>   I will surely have mercy on him,
>   says the LORD. (Jer. 31.20)

> When Israel was a child, I loved him,
>   and out of Egypt I called my son.
> The more I called them,
>   the more they went from me;
> they kept sacrificing to the Baals,
>   and offering incense to idols.
> Yet it was I who taught Ephraim to walk,
>   I took them up in my arms ...
> I led them with cords of human kindness,
>   with bands of love ...

How can I give you up, Ephraim?
How can I hand you over, O Israel? ...
My heart recoils within me;
    my compassion grows warm and tender.

(Hos. 11.1–4a, 8)

As a father has compassion for his children,
    so the LORD has compassion for those who fear him.

(Ps. 103.13)

Israel, of course, was a patriarchal society so it is natural
that the preponderance of parental references in the Old
Testament is to God as Father. The idea of God's mother-
hood is not absent: 'I have calmed and quieted my soul,
like a weaned child with its mother ... O Israel, hope in
the LORD' (Ps. 131.2–3); 'Can a woman forget her nursing
child, or show no compassion for the child of her womb?
Even these may forget, yet I will not forget you' (Isa. 49.15).
Yet even the fatherly metaphors emphasize not some meta-
physical omnipotence or naked strength but God's stead-
fast love and effective care for his people, God's children.
It is vital that the biblical image of fatherhood should not
be distorted by any alien notions of sexism, Freudian psychology (God as a 'father figure') or of sentimental piety
(God as the benign but ineffectual 'old man in the sky'),
but rather that we allow the biblical image to govern our
understanding of the revealed nature of the living God.
According to its use in these contexts, it is neither sexual,
patriarchal nor oppressive. Whereas the pagan gods of the
ancient world were almost invariably sexual, Yahweh, the
God of Israel, creates alone; there is no subordinate female
principle within the deity.

There is in the doctrine of God's fatherhood no pagan attempt to assert masculinity at the expense of femininity.

> The love of God the Father ... is the original, although not the projection of all our human loves, and fulfils and holds together inside itself, the authority of father, but the tender care of mother also.[5]

In other words, although God is often referred to as 'he', God is beyond sexuality and gender. The God of the Old Testament scriptures is not a manifestation of the deity of patriarchy, a cosmic projection of the male ego, but the covenant Lord who, in his tender mercy, hears the prayers of his people and sets them free.

The New Testament Corroboration

When we move to the New Testament, the concept of God as Father comes to the fore. By breaking Jewish convention and referring to God repeatedly as '[my] Father' – either the Greek word 'Pater' or the Aramaic 'Abba', the familiar term for father (Mark 14.36; Matt. 26.39, 42; Luke 22.42 etc.) – and, while guarding the uniqueness of his own filial relationship to God, teaching his disciples to do likewise: 'When you pray say: Father, hallowed be your name' (Luke 11.1), Jesus ensured that the description of God as Father would become fundamental for Christian faith. Reference to God as Father is made incessantly in both the Gospels (150 times) and the Epistles (40 times), while the ultimate task of both the Son and the Holy Spirit is to bear witness to the Father: 'And this is eternal life, that they may know you, the only true God, and Jesus Christ whom you have sent' (John 17.3); 'For through him both of us have access in one Spirit to the *Father*' (Eph. 2.18). This is the same Father who disclosed himself to the people of Israel

---

5 Thomas A. Smail, *The Forgotten Father* (London: Hodder & Stoughton, 1980), pp. 58–9.

in the Old Testament (see Mark 12.26; Acts 5.30; Rom. 3.29). He possesses the same qualities: generosity (Matt. 7.11), mercy (Luke 6.36; 18.14), faithfulness and forgiveness (1 John 1.9), paternal love (1 John 3.1), eternal care (1 John 4.15). As Father he commands his people to be loving as he is loving, merciful as he is merciful, forgiving as he is forgiving, and perfect as he is perfect (Matt. 5.44–48; 18.32–35; Luke 6.36). He is 'the God and *Father* of our Lord Jesus Christ' who has chosen his people 'to be holy and blameless before *him*' (Eph. 1.3–4). It is their task to bear witness to the fact that he has sent Jesus into the world for the salvation of all people: 'And we have seen and do testify that the *Father* has sent his Son as the Saviour of the world' (1 John 4.14).

This God and Father retains both personhood and transcendence which are now qualified by the mediation of Jesus Christ. Yet the functions of God in Christ remain as the functions of Yahweh had been in the Old Testament: 'There is no significant difference between the God and Father we meet in the New Testament and Yahweh, the God of Israel, in the Old.'[6] Whereas under the former scheme the focus of God's dealings with men and women had been the patriarchs and the prophets of Israel, under the new arrangement it is Jesus, and in the ongoing life of the church, Jesus through the Holy Spirit. In the New Testament God is constantly referred to as 'God and Father of our Lord Jesus Christ' (Rom. 15.6; 2 Cor. 1.3; 11.38).

Christ, therefore, makes God known as Father; by implication he is the incarnate Son. By revealing God as his eternal Father, Christ says something not only about his relationship with God (and, by extension, of who God is to us) but also about who God is in himself. The thrust of the biblical evidence is that God's fatherhood belongs to

6 Christopher B. Kaiser, *The Doctrine of God* (London: Marshall, Morgan & Scott, 1982), p. 24.

the essence of what it means to be God; that God's father-hood is eternal. What God is to Jesus is what God is in the essence of his being. In the words of the Scottish theologian Thomas F. Torrance:

> By revealing himself in the Lord Jesus Christ as *his* dear Son, God reveals that Fatherhood belongs to his eter-nal Being, and in giving his Son to be the Saviour of the world, he reveals that he loves us to the uttermost with an eternal Fatherly love.[7]

This knowledge of God was first set forth in the Old Testa-ment and was intensified, found a focus and made manifest in Christ who was eternally Son to *this* Father. It was not so much that Jesus of Nazareth experienced God, that on the basis of this experience that he called God 'Father' and then bid his followers to do likewise. Rather, the father-hood which Christ as the only-begotten Son revealed to humankind already belonged to who God was in himself. He was 'the Father, from whom every family in heaven and on earth takes his name' (Eph. 3.15) and not vice versa; God's fatherhood is not a projection of human experience but the basis and archetype of what all human fatherhood should be. What is more, by making known this Father, Christ also revealed the nature of the relationship between God and those who would, through faith, be united with him: 'For you did not receive a spirit of slavery to fall back into fear, but you have received a spirit of adoption. When we cry "Abba! Father" it is that very Spirit bearing witness that we are children of God' (Rom. 8.15–16). This spirit of adoption, which seals our relationship with God as child-ren of the heavenly Father, makes God real to us and is the basis of our own life in Christ: 'Because you are children,

7 Thomas F. Torrance, *The Christian Doctrine of God: One Being, Three Persons* (Edinburgh: T & T Clark, 1996), p. 55.

God has sent the Spirit of his Son into our hearts, crying "Abba! Father!"' (Gal. 4.6). All this implies that there is an eternal bond or unity between God as Father, Son and Holy Spirit and that the titles 'Father', 'Son' and 'Spirit' are not incidental aspects of some abstract essence called 'God', but that God *is* Father, Son and Holy Spirit in the very depths of his being. The profound implications of this for our faith will become clear, I hope, as we proceed.

By referring to God as Father, therefore, the Christian community has merely followed the example and instruction of Jesus Christ, its Lord. The father image is not a simple human personification, a man-made anthropomorphism, but a true reflection of God's own self-revelation as mediated through Christ. It was Jesus who claimed: 'All things have been handed over to me; and no one knows the Son except the Father, and no one knows the Father except the Son and anyone to whom the Son chooses to reveal him' (Matt. 11.27). We are invited to call God our Father and enter into fellowship with him having been so bidden by Christ, the Father's eternal Son and our Lord.

God the Creator

'It has always been of decisive importance for Christianity that the God who liberates and redeems is none other than the creator of the world.'[8] Both the Old Testament and the New express this continuum between redemption and creation. God redeems by recreating men and women and their world. He does this partially and proleptically (that is, in anticipation of the end time) on the basis of faith here and now, and will do so finally and fully with the consummation of all things at the close of history. Christ

---

8 Wolfhart Pannenberg, *The Apostles' Creed in the Light of Today's Questions* (London: SCM Press, 1972), p. 36.

is the second Adam, and humanity, redeemed in Christ, is humanity restored to its original state. The Father God who is redeemer and the Father God who is creator are one and the same.

God's work as creator is universally expressed in scripture. Apart from the actual creation narratives in the Book of Genesis (Gen. 1–2), the conviction that God created the world is expressed by the psalmist:

> Before the mountains were brought forth,
>> or ever you had formed the earth and the world,
>> from everlasting to everlasting you are God.
>>> (Ps. 90.2; cf. 102.25–26)

by the prophets:

> Lift up your eyes on high and see:
>> Who created these?
> He who brings out their host and numbers them,
>> calling them all by name;
> because he is great in strength,
>> mighty in power ...
> Have you not known? Have you not heard?
> The LORD is the everlasting God,
>> the Creator of the ends of the earth.
>>> (Isa. 40.26, 28; cf. Jer. 10.12–13; Amos 4.13)

by the evangelists:

> All things came into being through him, and without him not one thing came into being. (John 1.3)

and by the apostles:

> For in him all things in heaven and on earth were created, things visible and invisible ... all things have been

created through him and for him' (Col. 1.16; cf. Rev. 4.11; 10.16)

The classic account of creation in Genesis 1—2 states that God first created the heavens and the earth, that they were without form and void, and that there was a brooding darkness on the face of the deep. From this primeval chaos God created order and harmony, in other words a cosmos. This creation was absolute, *ex nihilo* ('out of nothing'). It was not fashioned out of pre-existent matter, like a carpenter fashioning a piece of furniture from a block of wood, for then matter would have been co-eternal with God. This would imply the existence of a dualistic universe with two basic and competing principles, God and matter, the one being in opposition to the other. Neither was the creation an extension or emanation of God himself. Were this the case, the distinction between God and the world would be blurred and the creation itself would be divine. The early Christian theologians realized that each alternative would have been fatal for the integrity of Christian truth and so devised the doctrine of creation *ex nihilo* in order to safeguard both the absolute nature of the biblical God and to preserve the distinct character of the material creation. Although both ideas have their roots in antiquity, they are still very prevalent today and present a challenge for the current health of the church just as much as they did centuries ago. Perhaps we should explore the subject further.

Pre-Christian thought believed that the universe had no beginning and, presumably, would have no end; it was eternal and as such it, and not God, embodied the ultimate reality. The deities of the classical world were neither omnipotent nor particularly holy, and all they could do was to influence the world in some way. According to the Reformed theologian Colin E. Gunton: 'The ideal that a personal God should create everything there is was simply not conceivable until the Christian gospel's theologians came along.'[9] The Hebrew scriptures had already conveyed Israel's unshakeable conviction that Yahweh was the true God, awe-ful in power, who was the creator of the world. When the Christian church commended the truth that God was not only the absolute creator and as such different from creation, but that creation possessed an integrity of its own, both dualistic and monistic interpretations of reality were challenged in a radical way. The idea of creation *ex nihilo* had no analogy in ancient belief. It was, in fact, 'a distinctive piece of teaching, unique in the history of thought, and deriving from the challenge presented to the church by the culture of the world in which it lived'.[10] Much of that culture had a negative view of all created reality; matter, although eternal, was bad. Only the realm of the spirit was good, and the religious quest consisted in extracting oneself from the realm of matter towards some pure ethereal plane. This, of course, was absolutely contrary to the conviction of scripture. The world was created by God, and as such it was wholly *good*. 'The most obtrusive feature of the priestly creation narrative is the drumbeat rhythm of the six days: indeed this is the chief means by which this subtly reflected document, the product of a rhetorically sophisticated society, does its teaching.'[11] Seven times does that rhythm beat out the sonorous phrase: 'And God saw that it was *good*' (Gen. 1.4, 10, 12, 18, 21, 25, 31). Not only is God different from creation as its creator and Lord, but as the good creator God has imbued creation with a reflection of the divine goodness. No one need extricate himself or herself from it in order to know God. Although different from creation, God deems creation to be good.

---

9 Gunton, *The Christian Faith*, p. 17.
10 Gunton, *The Christian Faith*, p. 17.
11 Robert W. Jenson, *Systematic Theology* vol. 2, *The Works of God* (New York: Oxford University Press, 1997), p. 5.

Dualism, or the idea that creation is somehow evil, has always been attractive to the religious imagination and often it has impacted adversely on Christian faith. 'Consider', writes the Princeton theologian Daniel L. Migliore, 'some of the forms it has taken and continues to take':

> The spiritual is good, the physical is evil; the intellectaul is good, the sexual is evil; the masculine is good, the feminine is evil; white is good, black is evil; human beings are good, the natural environment is evil. Over against such dualisms, Christian faith declares that all God has created is good. To regard any part of creation as inherently evil – the Manichean heresy – is both slanderous and destructive.[12]

In other words, God's creation is good, matter is not intrinsically evil, the physical world was made by God for his glory and affirmed by Christ who was God incarnate, that is, God in material, tangible, created form. The only duality to which Christianity admits is that between sin and grace and not between God and matter, or the soul and the body, or the 'spiritual' and the physical.

But it may be that it is not dualism which is the main challenge to Christianity in the new millennium but monism, dualism's opposite. Monism, or pantheism, is the idea that creation and God are of a piece or that the created universe is an extension of God. However sensitive we need to be to ecological concerns, and to the criticism that by driving a wedge between creation and creator, Christians have opened the way to exploiting the world rather than caring for it, we cannot blur the distinction between God and the world. To deify creation, as is popular with many contemporary 'creation spiritualities', causes huge perplex-

---

12 Daniel L. Migliore, *Faith Seeking Understanding: An Introduction to Christian Theology* (Grand Rapids: Eerdmans, 1991), p. 88.

ity: it undermines the difference between good and evil and right and wrong. Ultimately it robs creation of its rightful autonomy under God's sustaining word. Although God upholds the world by his power and grace, categorically God is different from the world. 'The first proposition [for a sound doctrine of creation is] that God creates ... other reality than God and that it is really other than he.'[13] God and the world should not be allowed to collapse into one another, for everyone's sake. If God retains transcendence, otherness and lordship, the world, as a created phenomenon, retains a validity and integrity of its own.

God's original activity in creation is continued in his sustaining power, God's upholding of the creation in the Word. And who was the Word? 'It did not take the New Testament writers long to identify God's creating Word with Jesus Christ, who is the Word who became part of the created order.'[14] Even before coming into the created order in Jesus of Nazareth, the divine Logos, creative principle or Word, is said to have been active in both the creation and sustenance of all things:

> In the beginning was the Word, and the Word was with God, and the Word was God. He was in the beginning with God. All things came into being through him, and without him not one thing came into being. (John 1.1–3; cf. 1 Cor. 8.6; Col. 1.17)

As 'the reflection of God's glory and the exact imprint of God's very being', it is the Logos or divine Son who 'sustains all things by his powerful word' (Heb. 1.3). In other words, it is through Christ that God manifests his common grace towards humankind. The Bible itself refers to the order of the stars and the seasons (Job 38.31–33; Isa.

---

13 Jenson, *The Works of God*, p. 5.
14 Gunton, *The Christian Faith*, p. 9.

40.26; Acts 14.17), the bounty of crops and the benevolence of harvests (Deut. 11.10–12; Ps. 104.14–23; Hos. 2.8). It emphasizes constantly God's manifold goodness to humankind:

> Consider the lilies of the field, how they grow; they neither toil nor spin, yet I tell you, even Solomon in all his glory was not clothed like one of these. But if God so clothes the grass of the fields, which is alive today and tomorrow is thrown into the oven, will he not much more clothe you? (Matt. 6.28–30)

It is this miracle of creation and preservation to which the 'goodness' of the Genesis narrative refers. In the words of Dietrich Bonhoeffer:

> That which was created by the Word out of nothing, and that which is called forth into being, remains sustained by the sight of God. It does not sink back again into the moment of becoming; God sees that it is good and his eyes, resting upon the work, preserves that work in being. Therefore the world is preserved by the one who is its Creator and alone for the one who is its Creator. The world is preserved not for its own sake but for the sake of the sight of God.[15]

Knowledge of God the creator stems from knowledge of God the Son for it was through the Son that all things were made and it is in him that all things hold together (John 1.10; Col. 1.17). God's omnipotence is an obvious corollary

---

15 Dietrich Bonhoeffer, *Creation and Fall: A Theological Interpretation of Genesis 1–3* (New York: Macmillan, 1959), p. 26; for a newer translation see idem. *Creation and Fall: A Theological Exposition of Genesis 1–3*, *Dietrich Bonhoeffer Works* vol. 3 (Minneapolis: Fortress Press, 1997), p. 47.

of this fact but it must always be understood christological-ly, that is, in the light of Christ, rather than speculatively or in any abstract or theoretical way. The fact that Christ, the eternal Word, is deemed to be the source of God's creative and sustaining activity within the world, and that God, the Holy Spirit, is seen as the means by which the divine comes upon creation, must always control this concept of omnipotence. The inexpressible might which both created and upholds the world manifested itself, in the fullness of time, in the Son's condescension when he took upon himself the flesh of frail humanity:

> who, though he was in the form of God,
>> did not regard equality with God
>> as something to be exploited,
> but emptied himself,
>> taking the form of a slave,
>> being born in human likeness.
> And being found in human form,
>> he humbled himself
>> and became obedient to the point of death
>> even death on a cross. (Phil. 2.6–8)

That the almighty God should so humble himself by becoming incarnate in the helpless babe of Bethlehem and the 'man of sorrows' upon the cross, all the while retaining his essential deity, constituted an act of such stupendous majesty and power that it all but defies human comprehension. Yet in Christ this is what happened: 'God is not proud. In his high majesty he is humble.'[16] It is because of that incarnate weakness and divine brokenness that God's omnipotence can never be understood in terms of arbitrary power or naked force. It is, rather, the omnipotence of the

---

16 Karl Barth, *Church Dogmatics* IV/1, *The Doctrine of Reconciliation* (Edinburgh: T & T Clark, 1956), p. 159.

crucified God, the strength of the eternal Word made perfect in weakness:

> Therefore God also highly exalted him
>   and gave him the name
>   that is above every name,
> so that at the name of Jesus
>   every knee should bend,
>   in heaven and on earth and under the earth,
> and every tongue should confess
>   that Jesus Christ is Lord,
>   to the glory of God the Father. (Phil. 2.9–11)

Questions for Discussion

1 What is the significance of regarding God as personal?

2 Why do we refer to God as Father, not Mother? Would it make any difference were we to use language that was not gender-specific to refer to God?

3 Explain the link between God as creator and God as saviour or redeemer.

4 How would you go about developing a 'green' theology?

5 Should Christians embrace or reject pantheism or 'creation spirituality'?

6 What is the place of Jesus Christ in a Christian understanding of creation?

4

The Christian Doctrine of God
The Holy Trinity

Jesus as God

It was the universal Old Testament conviction that there was but one God and that God was Yahweh, the Creator-Redeemer God who had revealed himself to Israel. But with the advent of Jesus, a new and revolutionary situation arose which required an extension of the original doctrine. For if Yahweh was the one and only true God, Jesus displayed attributes remarkably similar to those of the Father. Christians found themselves experiencing God not only as the eternal Father but as the divine Son. It was this dilemma that led the church to devise a formula that would both safeguard the unity or 'oneness' of God and do justice to the divinity of Jesus. What is more, following Christ's resurrection and ascension to glory, the Christian community's experience of its Lord – that is, the one God as Father and Son – had now to be mediated in a further way, through the Spirit. And if God must reveal himself immediately and not secondarily to his people – in the words of Karl Barth: 'God, the Revealer, is identical with His act in revelation and also identical with its effect'[1] – the Spirit too would have to be considered divine. It was a logic such as this, based upon the New Testament church's actual *experience*

---

1 Karl Barth, *Church Dogmatics* I/1, *The Doctrine of the Word of God* (Edinburgh: T & T Clark, 1975), p. 296.

of God in Christ, that led to the formulation of the doctrine of the Trinity.

Both the New Testament Gospels and the Epistles identify Jesus with Yahweh, the one true Lord and God. In Mark 1, for instance, Jesus is introduced in yahwistic language as the 'Lord' whose appearance was prepared for by John the Baptist (Mark 1.2–3; cf. Isa. 40.3). In chapter 2, Mark makes a point of Jesus' 'authority on earth to forgive sins' in terms that are equally yahwistic: 'Who can forgive sins but God alone?' (2.7, 10; cf. Ps. 65.2–3). In chapter 3, Jesus gathers the twelve disciples to be with him (3.14); the twelve constitute a representative regathering of the twelve tribes of Israel (see Num. 1—4). Chapter 4 depicts Jesus' revelation of himself as lord of the elements. Just as the sailor described by the psalmist turns to God in Psalm 107.28, so the storm-tossed disciples here turn to Jesus at whose command the elements respond and become calm (4.39; cf. Ps. 65.7; 89.9; 107.29): 'Who then is this', they ask, 'that even the wind and the sea obey him?' (4.41). As it was God's prerogative in the Old Testament to rule the elements, so Jesus here displays an authority which is divine. In the fifth chapter we read of the raising of Jairus' daughter from 'the point of death' (5.23; cf. Ps. 107.17–20) accompanied by the words of assurance, so often spoken by God in the Old Testament, 'Do not fear' (5.36; cf. Exod. 20.20; Deut. 31.6, 8; Isa. 41.10). In chapter 6 Jesus feeds the hungry in a 'deserted place' (6.36), just as God had fed the children of Israel in the wilderness (cf. Ps. 107.4–7), while his miracle of walking on the water (6.47–51) is a clear echo of God's own jurisdiction once more over the elements: 'Take heart, it is I; do not be afraid' (6.50; cf. Isa. 51.12–16). In the seventh chapter, the Gentile woman whose daughter was possessed by an unclean spirit refers specifically to Jesus as '*Kurie*', the Greek word which, although translated as 'Sir', means 'Lord' (7.28), and displays her faith in him, while the climax of this development occurs in chapter 8 when Peter explicitly confesses his faith in Jesus as the Christ: 'He asked them, "But who do you say that I am?" Peter answered him, "You are the Messiah"' (8.29). So throughout these initial chapters in what is regarded as being the earliest of the New Testament Gospels, Jesus is identified as Yahweh, the Old Testament's one single God.

The Gospels, however, do not represent the oldest strata in New Testament literature. That position belongs to the Epistles. Again the universal conviction of the letters attributed to the apostle Paul (and the others) is that this time the *risen* Christ is to be identified with Yahweh, the eternal Lord. The first of these references is to be found in the very earliest of the New Testament Epistles, 1 and 2 Thessalonians, which were written about AD 50. For instance 1 Thessalonians 3.13, 'at the coming of our Lord *Jesus* with all his saints', echoes the words of the prohet Zechariah in the Old Testament, 'the Lord *my God* shall come and all his saints with him' (Zech. 14.5). Thus, in regard to his second coming, Jesus is identified with the same Lord whose coming was awaited by Zechariah (cf. 1 Thess. 4.16 with Ps. 47.5). In 2 Thessalonians Jesus is further described as the one who will vindicate his people as God had promised to vindicate Israel of old (cf. 2 Thess. 1.6 with Isa. 66.15; 1.9 with Isa. 2.19; 1.12 with Isa. 24.15). In 1 and 2 Corinthians, written a few years later in AD 55, Paul makes his confession that 'Jesus is Lord' – 'no one can say "Jesus is Lord" except by the Holy Spirit' (1 Cor. 12.3) – which became, in turn, the basis for the second article in the classic Christian creeds, 'I believe in Jesus Christ his only Son our Lord'. It is apparent here, as elsewhere in the Corinthian letters, that Paul identifies the risen Christ with Yahweh and that the attributes and characteristics of the God of Israel are shared by Jesus Christ, the Son (1 Cor. 1.30–31;

2.16; 10.16–22; 2 Cor. 3.15; 10.17–18). Where does this lead us?

> We conclude that the fundamental Christian confession 'Jesus is Lord' is rooted in the recognition that the risen Christ is Yahweh, the God of Israel. This identification goes back to the day of Pentecost when Peter cited the same promise of Joel referred to by Paul in Romans 10.13 ('Whoever calls on the name of the Lord shall be saved' Joel 2.32) to explain the significance of baptism 'in the name of Jesus Christ' (Acts 2.16–40). The power and joy associated with the name of Jesus throughout the book of Acts stems from this identification of Jesus with Yahweh.[2]

So, in both Paul and Acts, Jesus' name takes the place of Yahweh as the one upon whom the believer may call for salvation (Acts 4.12). Having ascended to God's right hand, Jesus is now in a position to answer his people's prayers and grant them the gift of the Spirit: 'Therefore it is said, "When he [Yahweh] ascended on high he made captivity itself a captive; he gave gifts to his people"' (Eph. 4.8, quoting Ps. 68.18). From his resurrection, his ascension to his return in glory, Jesus is identified as Yahweh, the God of Israel.

This identification between Jesus and Yahweh is always qualified by a necessary distinction between the two. Jesus is always portrayed as being more than an adjunct of the one true God. He possesses a separate personhood although fully conjoined with God himself. The usual way in which the New Testament writers express this unity is in terms of sonship. There is but one God who possesses two separate foci of being, the one as the eternal God and

---

2 Christopher B. Kaiser, *The Doctrine of God* (London: Marshall, Morgan & Scott, 1982), pp.33–4.

heavenly Father and the other as the divine Son who took upon himself the form of a servant and came into the world as a human being like ourselves:

> It is through the action of the Spirit upon the common stuff of our humanity which the Son took to himself that it becomes *capax Dei*, capable of being joined in one person to the Son of God, who is himself in his eternal relation to the Father both recipient and donor of the Spirit.[3]

So God's original revelation as Father remained but was complemented by God's subsequent incarnation or enfleshment in Christ, the eternal Son (see Matt. 16.16; Heb. 4.14; Acts 8.37).

As Son of God, Jesus was fully personal, an integral part of God's being, yet distinct from the Father and capable of reciprocating the Father's love towards him in trust and obedience. It is in the Gospel of John that this relationship is most carefully worked out. It is seen there as being a relationship of distinctiveness within unity: 'What my Father has given me is greater than all else ... The Father and I are one' (John 10.29; cf. 14.28; 17.11, 22); it is a relationship of parity: 'My Father is still working, and I am still working' (John 5.17 and other parallels, e.g. 5.23 and 14.23; 1 John 1.3; 2.23); this parity is qualified only by the Son's obedience to and dependence upon the Father: 'For just as the Father has life in himself, so he has granted the Son also to have life in himself' (John 5.26; cf. 5.19); yet this element of obedience does not impinge on the Son's full sharing of the Father's nature: 'The Father is in me and I am in the Father' (John 10.38; cf. 10.15; 14.10–11, 20; 17.1, 21). In these expressions, the author of John's gospel combines precision of

---

3 Tom Smail, *The Giving Gift: The Holy Spirit in Person*, 2nd edn (London: Darton, Longman & Todd, 1994), p. 94.

language with a sensitivity to interpersonal relations within the being or essence of God. The Son is distinct from the Father yet dependent upon the Father, yet both Father and Son are one God. According to Arthur Wainwright:

> The idea of Father and Son was the most fitted to account for the interaction within the Godhead. It could ... express how both Father and Son were God. It could point to the priority of the Father without detracting from the divinity of the Son. And finally it could account for the unity of the two persons.[4]

There is little doubt, on the basis of the New Testament evidence, that Jesus was regarded as being divine.

The Role of the Spirit

During Old Testament times the Spirit of Yahweh had on many occasions descended upon women and men. The Spirit first appears in the creation narrative (Gen. 1.1) and subsequently as the spirit which, coming directly from on high, enabled the servants of God, the judges and prophets and kings, to fulfil the divine will (e.g. Judg. 3.10, 6.34; 1 Sam. 16.13; 1 Chron. 12.18 etc.). So when the Spirit of Pentecost came upon the church, the New Testament writers identified that spirit with the previously revealed spirit of God (Acts 2.16–21; 4.25–26; 28.25–28; Heb. 3.7–11; 1 Pet. 1.10–12). This continuity between the spirit in both testaments found a focus in the person of Jesus. Just as the creator spirit of the Old Testament had hovered over the primeval waters of chaos, so in the New Testament the Spirit had descended upon Jesus during his baptism in the

---

4 Arthur Wainwright, *The Trinity in the New Testament*, 4th edn (London: SPCK, 1977), p. 263.

waters of Jordan. It was the same spirit that had been active in his conception through Mary, the blessed Virgin, in his baptism by John and in his resurrection from the dead. Subsequently it was the Spirit who would direct the mission of the church after Jesus' ascension into heaven following his resurrection from the dead (Matt. 1.20; 3.16; Rom. 1.4; Acts 3.23; 8.9).

Unlike Jesus, in the New Testament the Spirit is never directly identified with Yahweh or explicitly referred to as God. Rather the Spirit's ministry is to point towards the risen Christ and the person of the Father: 'But the Advocate (*Paraclētos*), the Holy Spirit, whom the Father will send in my name, will ... remind you of all that I have said to you' (John 14.26; cf. 15.26); 'He [the Spirit of truth] will glorify me' (John 16.14). Although universally present in the New Testament, the Spirit is so in association with Christ having been sent by the Father; that is, the Spirit does not exist independently of either Father or Son. Such was the nature of this association that the reflection of the church would lead it to the inevitable conclusion that the Spirit, while possessing a personhood or identity of his own, shared deity with both Father and the Son. In other words, the Spirit too must be divine. The Spirit's name was always included with the name of the Father and the Son. The words of 'the grace' in 2 Corinthians 13.13; the threefold confession of faith in 'one Spirit, one Lord and one Father' of Ephesians 4.4–6, as well as the baptismal formula 'in the name of the Father and of the Son and of the Holy Spirit' in Matthew 28.19, indicate the intrinsic nature of the Spirit's divine role in early Christian faith and experience. The Spirit's function within these formulae did not detract from the unity of the one God as Father and Son (Eph. 2.18; John 14.16–23), rather it was seen to complement both the ministry of the Father (1 Cor. 6.19; 1 John 3.24; 4.16) and that of the Son (Rom. 8.9–11; 1 Cor. 2.12–16). And as Jesus had parity with the Father so the Spirit too has equality with both Father and Son. As 'no one knows that Father except the Son', so 'no one comprehends what is truly God's except the Spirit of God' (Matt. 11.27; 1 Cor. 2.11). So, 'when the Advocate (*Paraclētos*) comes, whom I will send to you from the Father, the Spirit of truth who comes from the Father, he will testify on my behalf' (John 15.26). Whereas God the Father retains priority within the Godhead, the subordination of the divine and eternal Son and the sending forth of the divine and eternal Spirit do not imply an inferiority of status or a difference in substance. Rather, *both* were sent by God (Gal. 4.4–6) for the purpose of glorifying the Father in the salvation of humankind, and *both* participate fully in God's very being. As Christopher Kaiser has written:

> If the Church had concluded that Jesus was merely a man, then it might have regarded the Spirit as a mere force. But once it concluded that Jesus was of the same nature as God the Father, it could not but have regarded the Spirit as of the very same nature as father and Son.[5]

It was on the basis of these convictions – that the one true God, Yahweh, had revealed himself as Father Almighty; that, in the fullness of time, he had revealed himself in Christ, the only-begotten (if eternal) Son of the Father who became flesh for the salvation of humankind; and thirdly as the divine (and still eternal) Spirit who, among other things, animated the church and progressively sanctifed all of God's people – that the church's classic doctrine of the Trinity was devised.

---

5 Kaiser, *The Doctrine of God,* p. 43.

A Doctrine of Trinity and Its Implications

Because the church worshipped *this* God, the heavenly Father who had been so revealed by the eternal Son through the divine Spirit; the eternal Son who had offered himself in perfect obedience to the Father in order to atone for the sins of the world; the divine Spirit who proceeded from the Father in order constantly to renew humanity and the whole of creation in the image of the Son; because of this, the theologians of the early church set about the task of formulating their experience of God in strictly trinitarian terms.

The word 'trinity' does not appear in the Bible, neither does the developed doctrine of the Trinity with its rather technical expressions of one 'substance' (*ousia*) in three 'persons' (*personae* or *hypostasia*). What does appear in scripture, as we have seen, is a triadic or threefold description of the way that God functions in the world as Father, Son and Holy Spirit – what the theologians would come to describe as the 'economic Trinity' (from the Greek word for 'order' or 'plan') – which would invariably imply much about who God was in his essence or at the core of his being – what theology would come to call the 'immanent Trinity', what God was in himself. Far from being alien corruptions spoiling the simplicity of faith, what this technical terminology did was to provide the church with a precise mode of speech which drew out the deeper meaning of scripture and did justice to how Christians worshipped and to that which they actually believed. Whereas sometimes the *words* of scripture, either those used by Paul to the Romans or the Corinthians or of John in his account of the gospel of Christ, could be read in a way that subordinated the Son to the Father in a radical way or failed to express the full divinity of the Spirit, the inner consistency of the gospel story led the church to confess the reality of the one

God in three separate persons. As the words of the great Creed, formulated by the Council of Nicaea AD 325 and reaffirmed by the Council of Constantinople in AD 381, stated:

> We believe in one God, the Father almighty, maker of heaven and earth, of all things visible and invisible; and in one Lord Jesus Christ, begotten from the Father before all ages, light from light, true God from true God, begotten not made, of one substance with the Father ... And in the Holy Spirit, the Lord and life-giver, who proceeds from the Father, who with the Father and the Son is together worshipped and together glorified ...[6]

Whereas the Roman theologian Sabellius (*fl. c.* 210–30) had claimed that the Father, Son and Spirit were merely three different aspects or manifestations of the one single God and did not possess personhood as such, and the Alexandrian cleric Arius (d. 336) had insisted that the Son did not share full deity with the Father, there were those who were convinced that neither of these constructs did justice to the reality of the faith or to their evangelical experience of salvation in Christ. After much thought and prayer, the leaders of the church, first at the Council of Nicaea and then at the Council of Constantinople, made their deliberation: that the Christian God was one God in three persons, each sharing the same nature with one another and each relating to one another, the Father as the source or fount (*archē*) of the Godhead, the Son 'eternally begotten of the Father' and perpetually obedient to him, and the Spirit proceeding from the Father and responding constantly to both Father and Son. God, therefore, was not a solitary monad but three interconnected 'persons', each indwelling

6 J. N. D. Kelly, *Early Christian Creeds*, 3rd edn (London: Longman, 1972), pp. 297–8.

the other and fulfilling their unified, if separate, functions. In the words of the Protestant Reformer John Calvin over a thousand years after the great church councils, though in wholesale continuity with them:

> To the Father is attributed the beginning of activity, and the fountain and well-spring of all things; to the Son, wisdom, counsel and the ordered disposition of all things; but to the Spirit is assigned the power and efficacy of that activity.[7]

Thus was formulated the church's doctrine of the Trinity.

But what are its implications for us today?

For worship – and all true theology begins and ends in worship, doxology, adoration and praise – it ensures that we are in union with Christ and partake of the redemption which has been acheived for humankind through his sacrifice on the cross, and what he continues to do on our behalf in his perpetual mediation at the right hand of the Father, and in his ongoing mission in the world:

> For you did not receive a spirit of slavery to fall back into fear, but you have received a spirit of adoption. When we cry 'Abba! Father!' it is that very Spirit bearing witness with our spirits that we are children of God, and if children, then heirs, heirs of God and joint heirs with Christ. (Rom. 8.15–17)

This is the basis of all true worship, rooted in the sheer grace of God as set forth in Christ on the cross and shed abroad in our hearts by the Holy Spirit. The cerebral moralism of so much conventional Christian worship which treats Christ as a mere example to follow and seems bereft

---

7 John Calvin, *Institutes of the Christian Religion* 1.13.18 (Philadelphia: Westminster Press, 1960), pp. 142–3.

of the renewing presence of the Holy Spirit is a travesty of the living thing. The significance of trinitarianism for true Christian worship is absolute.

If men and women experience the fullness of their true humanity in worship, it follows that their very humanity bears the imprint of the Trinity. When God is envisaged in solitary terms, as monad rather than triad, God the sovereign individual as it were, exalted far above creation and a stranger to the reciprocal relation of love as displayed between Father, Son and Holy Spirit, the resulting concept of humankind will be solitary and individualistic. Since the eighteenth-century Enlightenment, much of our Christianity here in the West has been infected by this view, seeing God as transcendent Lord whose relationship with the world is more legal than gracious and who demands rational obedience from his subjects rather than mutual communion with his friends.

The doctrine of the Trinity, however, teaches that God exists as communion, therefore being itself, as created by God, is relational in its essence. To be is to exist in partnership, communion and mutuality with others. This is the great truth of personhood: a person is *not* an atomized individual but a being who exists in relation with another. This was the meaning of 'person' (*hypostasis*) as predicated to God: three persons each indwelling the other and relating appropriately within the divine being. So as God is personal, our own personhood is fulfilled in relation with our fellow human beings. Men and women, created by God and reflecting God's image, are not 'individuals' with inalienable 'rights' as much as persons who can only achieve ultimate fulfilment by denying self and serving one another. The postmodern cult of the individual with its often narcissistic obsession with self-esteem and self-fulfilment can only thrive when the trinitarian sense of God is lost and belief in

God's objective threefold being is rejected. True humanity blossoms in self-effacing communion with God and with our neighbours.

Neither is this bereft of political significance. To the extent that religion reflects a non-trinitarian, anti-communal concept of God, it is open to oppression from the top, a hierarchical abuse of political power. This is a theme that the influential Reformed theologian Jürgen Moltmann and the liberation theologians of South America and elsewhere, never tire of emphasizing: 'Religiously motivated political monotheism', claims Moltmann, 'has always been used in order to legitimize domination, from the emperor cults of the ancient world, Byzantium and the absolute ideologies of the seventeenth century, down to the dictatorships of the twentieth.'[8] He would probably extend this now to include radical Islamic states and their all-powerful western adversaries in the twenty-first century. For him, and other contemporary theologians as well, a trinitarian Christianity spells community, equality and freedom:

> The Christian doctrine of the Trinity unites God, the almighty Father, with Jesus the Son, whom he delivered up and whom the Romans crucified, and with the life-giving Spirit, who creates the new heaven and the new earth. It is impossible to form the figure of the omnipotent, universal monarch, who is reflected in earthly rulers, out of the unity of this Father, this Son and this Spirit.[9]

It is the one true God, Father, Son and Spirit, who can ensure humankind the freedom and equality which is our creaturely due.

---

8 Jürgen Moltmann, *The Trinity and the Kingdom of God* (London: SCM Press, 1981), p. 192.
9 Moltmann, *The Trinity*, p. 197.

Questions for Discussion

1 In what sense can we claim that Jesus Christ is divine?

2 Discuss the way in which the idea of one God as Trinity developed. Do you think that this development was reasonable or not?

3 What characteristics does a person possess? Does it make sense to call Father, Son and Spirit 'persons'?

4 How best would you describe the role of the Holy Spirit in your experience of God?

5 It has been claimed that 'The Trinity means that God is a community.' How, then, should this affect our attitude to community life today?

6 Discuss the implications of the verse: 'The grace of the Lord Jesus Christ, the love of God, and the communion of the Holy Spirit be with all of you' (2 Cor. 13.13).

5

Humanity – Created and Fallen

The Nature of Human Creaturehood

The first characteristic of humankind according to the Christian scheme is that it belongs to the realm of the created: men and women can only be understood in the context of creation. As there exists an explicit and qualitative difference between God and creation, so humankind, as part of that creation, exists on a different level from that of God. On the horizontal level men and women have solidarity with the other created beings. There also exists a vertical dimension to their lives; they possess a certain correspondence with God as having been created in God's image and likeness. If the other creatures are created 'after their kinds' (Gen. 1.24–25), humankind, both man and woman, is created by God 'in our image, according to our likeness' (Gen. 1.26). So humankind is first creaturely, though in a way that sets it apart from the other creatures. The gifts that mark the difference between humankind and other creatures ensue from the unique nature of this correspondence with God: 'The freedom of the Creator demonstrates itself by allowing us to be free, free for the Creator. That, however, means nothing else than that the Creator's image is created on earth.'[1] The scriptural account of humankind having been formed as the pinnacle of God's creation (Gen.

---

1 Dietrich Bonhoeffer, *Creation and Fall: A Theological Exposition of Genesis 1–3*, *Dietrich Bonhoeffer Works* vol. 3 (Minneapolis: Fortress Press, 1997), p. 63.

1.26–28) and of having been shaped from the dust of the earth and animated by God's spirit (Gen. 2.7), underlines both aspects of this created being; on the one hand there is a link with creation and then the link with the creator:

> When I look at your heavens, the work of your fingers,
>> the moon and the stars that you have established;
>> what are human beings that you are mindful of them,
>> mortals that you care for them?
> You have made them a little lower than God,
>> and crowned them with honour and glory. (Ps. 8.3–5)

The concept which is principally important for the development of a specifically Christian anthropology is that of the image of God or *imago Dei*. This concept has been the subject of much analysis and reinterpretation, especially during recent generations. For centuries it was thought that the phrase referred to the human capacity to reason. Unlike the animals, which were ruled by their lusts and were creatures of instinct, men and woman were blessed with the gift of rational thought. They could rise above their passions by the use of the mind. According to this view, the endowment or faculty of reason *was* the image of God in humankind. As well as being highly flattering to the more intellectually endowed, such an interpretation – which owed more to Greek philosophy than to the biblical norms – led to the severe individualization of faith and seriously underrated the practical, embodied and non-cognitive aspects of life: 'If the essence of being human is seen primarily in the process of abstract reasoning, a corresponding depreciation of the emotional and physical dimensions of human existence results.'[2] However the *imago Dei* is to be understood, it must include the realities of material and social being, in

---

2 Daniel L. Migliore, *Faith Seeking Understanding: An Introduction to Christian Theology* (Grand Rapids: Eerdmans, 1991), p. 121.

other words it must take the concepts of creation, incarnation and trinity much more seriously than it has done at some stages during the past. Daniel L. Migliore, whose words are quoted above, is worth listening to again:

> Human existence is embodied existence. We are psycho-physical unities, not disembodied spirits. We do not simply *have* bodies: we *are* our bodies. Human flourishing cannot be separated from the satisfaction of bodily needs. Moroever, human life is socially and historically embedded. We belong to particular societies, cultures, and historical epochs, and these help to define our human identity.[3]

This being the case, the image of God is not some abstract faculty of the soul or possession of the individual mind, but it must be involved in that which roots a person in a particular time, place and historical context, and reflects the reality of being part of the created world of matter and of flesh.

Although contemporary theologians have written a vast amount on this rich and complex subject, we shall confine ourselves to three suggestions: that the image of God in humankind includes the facts of encounter, freedom and responsibility.

Encounter

> Then God said, 'Let us make humankind in our image, according to our likeness; and let them have dominion over the fish of the sea, and over the birds of the air, and over the cattle, and over all the wild animals of the earth, and over every creeping thing that creeps upon the earth.'

3 Migliore, *Faith Seeking Understanding*, p. 124.

> So God created humankind in his image,
>   in the image of God he created them;
>   male and female he created them. (Gen. 1.26–27)

Humankind, according to this narrative, is made in '*our*' image, and that image includes both male and female. There is a plurality in God (it would be anachronistic to see in these Old Testament verses a fully developed concept of the Trinity though not inaccurate to understand them as a germinal reference to the doctrine) and a corresponding plurality in humankind as created by God. When Genesis 2.18 elaborates this point by stating that Adam's solitary existence 'is not good' and God thereupon provides 'him a helper as his partner', the implication is that the *imago Dei* finds completion and fulfilment in the interpersonal encounter, the relationship which ensues between people within community. As the self can only exist in encounter with another, so humankind, created in God's image, experiences the fulfilment of that image within the context of interpersonal encounter. This is the soil from which relationships can develop.

As with so much else in recent theology, it was the twentieth-century Swiss theologian Karl Barth who alerted interpreters to the need for a fresh and more relationally based exegesis of this key text:

> Is it not astonishing that again and again expositors have ignored the definitive explanation given by the text itself, and instead of reflecting on it pursued all kinds of arbitrarily invested interpretations of the *imago Dei*? ... Could anything be more obvious than to concede from this clear indication that the image and likeness of the being created by God signified existence in confrontation, that is in *this* confrontation, juxtaposition and con-

junction of man and man which (in this case) is that of male and female.[4]

It is this encounter which presupposes our neighbour's demand upon us, the demand of love, on which basis ethics are possible. As God exists in a reciprocal relationship of love – the loving encounter of the Father with the Son and the Son with the Spirit within the holy Trinity – and as God has revealed himself as the God who has encountered men and women in creation and redemption, it follows that they can respond both to God and to one another as persons whose existence reflects God's plurality. This encounter and ensuing relationship with one's fellow or neighbour is a fulfilment of the image of God within. So the first aspect of the *imago Dei* can be said to be encounter.

Freedom

Humankind, having been created in the beginning by the Word, 'Then God *said*, "Let us make humankind in our image, according to our likeness"', and in dependence upon the divine Word for existence, has freedom. This freedom is a distinctive component of the *imago Dei*. According to God's original plan for humankind as illustrated by the creation narratives in the Book of Genesis, and subsequently by the way in which Jesus of Nazareth lives his life in absolute harmony with God, freedom is expressed as a wholehearted and willing response to the Word. Not only does the man, according to the Genesis story, respond spontaneously to God but also to his partner, or fellow human being, and to the lush, created world which provides a context for their lives. The context itself is highly

---

4 Karl Barth, *Church Dogmatics* III/1, *The Doctrine of Creation* (Edinburgh: T & T Clark, 1958), p. 196.

significant. The image of God functions within the created, material realm which reflects God's wholesale goodness, benevolence and glory. The commandment to have dominion over the creatures (which is so offensive to the contemporary mind), or the cultural mandate to subdue all things, is not exploitative but responsible:

> God blessed them, and God said to them, 'Be fruitful and multiply, and fill the earth and subdue it; and have dominion over the fish of the sea and over the birds of the air and over every living thing that moves upon the earth.' (Gen. 1.28)

> You have given them dominion over the works of your hands;
>> you have put all things under their feet,
> all sheep and oxen and also the beasts of the field,
> the birds of the air, and the fish of the sea,
>> whatever passes along the paths of the seas. (Ps. 8.6–8)

Men and women are not free to pillage and plunder the earth but to exercise a creative stewardship over it. It is the *corruption* of the image and not the image itself that is responsible for the disharmony and rapacity that is at the root of our current ecological malaise. For the biblical writers the blight of the earth was a direct consequence of having rebelled against God and disregarded his rule:

> The earth dries up and withers,
>> the world languishes and withers;
>> the heavens languish together with the earth.
> The earth lies polluted under its inhabitants;
>> for they have transgressed laws,
>> violated the statutes,
>> broken the everlasting covenant. (Isa. 24.4–6)

But dominion, according to this ideal, is not a hierarchical concept where the creature blindly obeys the repressive divine will and, in turn, oppresses creation, but a harmonious partnership where God's creative power expresses itself through a willing and generous human mediation. 'There is no dominion', claimed Dietrich Bonhoeffer, 'without serving God; in losing the one humankind necessarily loses the other.'[5] This freedom by the Word, and responsibility to God within his rich material creation, is an essential part of the *imago Dei*: 'Human freedom for God and the other person and human freedom from the creature in dominion over it constitute the first human beings' likeness to God.'[6]

Humankind, in response to God's Word, is free. It transcends the realms of the merely creaturely. Human encounter with, and freedom for, God and neighbour lift men and women above the rest of creation though they always retain their intimate link with the other creatures of their world. As God, in his sovereign freedom, chooses in Christ to be for humankind (we will have more to say about this in Chapter 7), so the human person exists in the likeness of God to be free for God and for his or her fellows. This is a freedom in dependence, the freedom of the finite being upon the ultimate source of all life. It is not the 'freedom' of individual autonomy, the freedom to be one's own master and lord. Such freedom is merely bondage, bondage to self, to the ego. So having encountered one's fellow and in reciprocation having affirmed God's image in him or her, one is set free to serve them in community. This is the freedom implied by the *imago Dei*.

5 Bonhoeffer, *Creation and Fall*, p. 67.
6 Bonhoeffer, *Creation and Fall*, p. 67.

Responsibility

Despite humankind's solidarity with the rest of creation, it alone bears the imprint of the divine image. This privilege inevitably brings responsibility. On the sixth day, when God summoned man and woman into being, God immediately addressed them as those who had response-ability to him. This ability to respond, this 'hearing' of the Word of God, are both a distinctively human quality and a mark of the image of God. Neither creation as such nor any other creature within creation has this capacity personally for hearing and responding to the address of God. Although creation can, in its own way, praise God's glory, its worship is not personally responsive:

> The heavens are telling the glory of God;
>> and the firmament proclaims his handiwork.
> Day to day pours forth speech,
>> and night to night declares knowledge.
> There is no speech, nor are there words;
>> their voice is not heard;
> yet their voice goes out through all the earth,
>> and their words to the end of the world. (Ps. 19.1–4)

Hugely powerful their proclamation may be, nevertheless neither creation nor the mute creature can be held in moral accountability to God. The *human* creature is, however, responsible to him. 'Our specificity in comparison with the other animals', states the American Lutheran theologian, Robert W. Jenson, 'is that we are the ones addressed by God's moral word and so enabled to respond.'[7] This accountability, which implies a conscience that witnesses to moral realities before God, is an intrinsic part of the *imago Dei*. A denial of this responsibility is a denial of a

---

7 Robert W. Jenson, *Systematic Theology* vol. 2, *The Works of God* (New York: Oxford University Press, 1997), p. 58.

person's humanity. That is why a wilful disobedience to the Word of God or to the norms of God within creation is demeaning, a denial of humanity. Such disobedience is, in a profound sense, inhuman. It is humankind and not the creation in general that bears the imprint of God's image.

Christ in his humanity exemplified this responsibility and responsiveness and to the full. Not only does Jesus embody the descent into humanity of the divine Logos, the coming among us of God's Word, but he displays the full, willing and totally free response of the human creature to God's call. The gospel story tells how he lived his life in perfect harmony with the Father's will. His childhood obedience, his baptism in the Jordan by John, his temptation in the wilderness, his ministry in Galilee, his rejection by the people in Jerusalem, his agony in the garden and his passion and death, are all in full and costly accord with the divine will. This is the unanimous testimony of the gospel witnesses and it gave rise to the apostle's claim, 'being found in human form he humbled himself and became obedient to the point of death – even death on a cross' (Phil. 2.7–8). His was not the automatic response of a divine being who had no choice but to be perfect, but the costly obedience of unfeigned humanity: 'Although he was a Son, he learned obedience through what he suffered; and having been made perfect, he became the source of eternal salvation for all those who obey him' (Heb. 5.8). Without weakening in any way the conviction that in Christ the eternal Son of God made himself one with humanity, it is this *human* response of Jesus of Nazareth to the Father's will which constitutes his being the bearer of the divine image in its totality. It is *this* Christ 'who is the image (*eikōn*) of God' (2 Cor. 4.4) and who reflects the weak and imperfect divine icon which we bear to the full; it is he who is totally 'the image of the invisible God' (Col. 1.15).

We claim, therefore, that a combination of encounter,

freedom and responsibility contribute to the divine likeness or correspondence, the *imago Dei*, in humankind. This is not just a religious concept. It has profound implications for all human life: ecology, interpersonal relations, ethics and morals, psychology, sexuality and not least human dignity in general. Far from being speculative and impractical, this concept provides the basis for a highly relevant knowledge of self and of society as created, sustained and redeemed by the triune God.

The 'terrible aboriginal calamity'

The doctrine of creation leads, ominously, to the doctrine of the fall: humankind is central to both. From its original position of partnership and harmony with God, humankind, both man and woman, rebels and becomes estranged from God. The ensuing alienation is portrayed as being deep-seated and calamitous. Not only does humanity forfeit God's company but provokes his judgement and wrath (Gen. 3.22–24; Rom. 1.18). In John Henry Newman's memorable sentence: 'The human race is implicated in some terrible aboriginal calamity.' From love of God, men and women turn inward on themselves; we have, in Luther's phrase, a *cor curvum in se* ('a heart turned in on itself'). This manifests itself in wilful independence taking the place of humble obedience and proud self-assertiveness replacing an attitude of trust. Just as serious (and equally self-centred) is a feeble inability to fulfil God's intention; sin as inactivity, indolence, servility or inertia: 'An adequate doctrine of sin will recognize that sin against the grace of God is not only titanic, Luciferian rebellion but also the timid, obsequious refusal to dare to be fully human by God's grace.'[8] Theologically, the fall marks humankind's

---

8 Migliore, *Faith Seeking Understanding*, p. 131.

hopeless rift from God and our moral antipathy towards God; alternatively it marks God's forsaking of humankind which, mercifully, was not permanent or irrevocable.

This is the way in which Christianity has traditionally understood the human condition, and despite changes over the years in the way that scripture has been interpreted, the doctrine of the fall retains a unique potency to provide insights into the perpetual paradoxes of human existence. For the American thinker Reinhold Niebuhr, in a still classic account of the subject, 'The profundity of the account of the Fall in Genesis cannot be overestimated.'[9] According to the story, Adam and Eve are persuaded to defy God's will by a twofold argument. First they are tempted to refuse to believe God's word:

> The woman said to the serpent, 'We may eat of the fruit of the trees in the garden; but God said, "You shall not eat of the fruit of the tree that is in the middle of the garden, nor shall you touch it, or you shall die."' But the serpent said to the woman, 'You will not die.' (Gen. 3.2–4)

Second, they are tempted to pride: 'God knows that when you eat of it your eyes will be opened, and you will be like God, knowing good and evil' (Gen. 3.5). Although it is Eve who is the focus of the serpent's blandishments, both Adam and Eve partake fully in this original unbelief and fall. The male, too, is wilful and disobedient.

What are we to make of Adam and Eve? It is striking that the story is never mentioned in the Old Testament after the opening chapters in the Book of Genesis. Although the Hebrews knew only too well of the tragedy of their own sinfulness and had an often searing sense of transgression

---

9 Reinhold Niebuhr, *The Nature and Destiny of Man* vol. 1, *Human Nature* (London: James Nisbet, 1941), p. 253.

and guilt, they did not apparently consider these matters
in terms of Adam and Eve, much less in terms of inherited
guilt. Sinners they were, having been made conscious of
social unrighteousness (Isa. 1.12–18), personal unworthi-
ness (Isa. 6.1–8) and a corporate culpability that provoked
God's wrath (Isa. 59):

> Come now, let us argue it out, says the LORD.
> Though your sins are like scarlet,
>   they shall be like snow;
> though they are red like crimson,
>   they shall become like wool. (Isa. 1.18)

> Woe is me! I am lost, for I am a man of unclean lips, and
> I live among a people of unclean lips; yet my eyes have
> seen the King, the LORD of hosts. (Isa. 6.8)

> Your iniquities have been barriers
>   between you and your God,
> and your sins have hidden his face from you
>   so that he does not hear. (Isa. 59.2)

Yet the story of Adam and Eve is confined to the creation
narratives in Genesis, a document which, although situated
at the beginning of our Bibles, was in fact fashioned much
nearer the end of the Old Testament period and edited into
its present position at a later date. It was the work of the
apostle Paul, through his concept of redemption in Christ
and Christ as 'the second Adam' (Rom. 5.12–24; 1 Cor.
15.45), which introduced 'the doctrine of the fall' into
Christian theology and by so doing provided the church
with a means of making some perverse sense of the universal blight of sin.

Who, then, was Adam? Adam means, in fact, 'man',
humanity in its generic and collective sense and not the

first created human being. Such is the literal meaning of the text. As Colin E. Gunton says: 'We do not need to believe in a historical Adam because the biblical story is itself too subtle to require such a naive and literalist reading.'[10] Yet the solidarity of the human race 'in Adam' came to provide a key – within the canon of scripture and under the guidance of divine inspiration – for a rich and unique theological understanding of both the individual and society. It is because Adam was not a 'mere individual' but an embodiment of the whole of humanity that the universal malaise of sin could be accounted for (though never fully explained). Unbelief, pride, sin, guilt, self-assertion and its antithesis, a perverse and servile self-negation, in fact the evil and tragedy which so characterize the human condition, could now be accounted for and begun to be coped with. The race is marred, corrupt, fallen because of the sin of Adam. His fall was the fall of all of humankind. We all participated in Adam's tragedy (Rom. 5.12–24).

It is certainly possible, within the bounds of Christian orthodoxy, to think of Adam in a purely symbolic way. And yet! If the world was created in harmony with God but is now, quite patently, out of kilter with him, how – and when – did this happen? 'Hominids who do not yet invoke God cannot sin', claims Robert W. Jenson, but at some juncture, not *beyond* time, space and history but *within* time, space and history, those who were imbued with the divine image did, in fact, begin to transgress.

> The story told in the third chapter of Genesis is not a myth; it does not describe what always and never happens. It describes the historical first happening of what thereafter always happens; moreover, had it not

---

10 Colin E. Gunton, *The Christian Faith: An Introduction to Christian Doctrine* (Oxford: Blackwell, 2002), p. 61.

happened with the first humans it could not have happened at all ...

... Who were Adam and Eve? ... The answer must be: the first community of our biological ancestors who disobeyed God's command.[11]

The grim-sounding concomitant to the concept of 'original sin', the inbred perversity that mars even our best attempts at virtue, is 'total depravity'. This does not mean that every person is as bad as he or she can be, but that the corruption and pollution produced by sin extends to the whole of our nature and permeates all of our characteristics – will, mind and virtue. So even at its best, human goodness is tainted by self-interest. 'There is no sin as subtle as the sin of "goodness"',[12] wrote the great Congregational theologian J. S. Whale more than a generation ago, while Martin Luther King blended psychological insight with the rhetoric of a master preacher in his observation: 'A man may be self-centred in his self-denial and self-righteous in his self-sacrifice. His generosity may feed his ego and his piety his pride.'[13] 'Moral pride', noted Niebuhr, 'makes virtue the very vehicle of sin.'[14]

Some contemporary feminist theology, for its part, has been critical of the orthodox doctrine of sin on several counts. The idea of sin as unbelief and pride presupposes a patriarchal God who demands subservience rather than an egalitarian God who invites participation in the divine life. Pride, moreover, is chiefly a male phenomenon; it is men who have been guilty for the most part of hubris, arrogance, self-assertion and egotism; it is their will-to-power

---

11 Jenson, *Systematic Theology* vol. 2, *The Works of God*, p. 150.
12 J. S. Whale, *Christian Doctrine*, 4th edn (Cambridge: Cambridge University Press, 1976), p. 39.
13 Martin Luther King, *Strength to Love* (London: Fontana Books, 1969), p. 145.
14 Niebuhr, *The Nature and Destiny of Man* vol. 1, p. 212.

which has so often led to conflict and war. Female sin, at least the sin of those women who have suffered through the patriarchal structures of society, is more likely to manifest itself as self-abegnation than self-assertiveness, a negation of the ego rather than its inflation. The figure of Eve is the object of particular disapproval. The misogynist tradition of biblical patriarchalism has assigned to her the role of temptress, 'weaker vessel' and the scapegoat for sin. The more radical strands of the movement apart, what feminist theology has done is to alert the church to the dangers of an unconsciously masculine bias in its practice and teaching. Nevertheless, neither unbelief, pride nor self-assertiveness are exclusively male characteristics. Neither do passivity, over-docility and a servile spirit belong wholly to the female realm. Even when shorn of all ideological elements, the biblical doctrine retains its unique ability to account for the depth of human imperfection.

Despite this malaise, the image of God remains.

The fact that human beings sin does not mean that God ceases to be God, and therefore humans cease to be human. In this context, too, we must say that human kind does not accomplish a new creation by sinning. We cannot achieve any essential alteration of the human nature which we have been given. We can only shame this nature and ourselves. We can only bring ourselves into supreme peril.[15]

The image of God is not destroyed through sin but inverted, reversed, turned inside out. Humankind, after the fall, turns away from God, but it is God from whom it turns. 'Sin', as Karl Barth states, in another context, 'is a degenerate form of the covenant relation between the Creator

---

15 Karl Barth, *Church Dogmatics* III/2, *The Doctrine of Creation* (Edinburgh: T & T Clark, 1960), p. 227, translation revised.

and the creature.'[16] So, instead of an encounter which leads to a responsible relationship within the community of humankind, sinful men and women manifest the divine image in self-contained loneliness or else an impaired or manipulative and egotistical relationship with others. Freedom for God becomes that parody of freedom, which is, in fact, bondage – freedom for self. Dominion over creation becomes exploitation of creation (cf. Isa. 24.4–5), and responsibility to God becomes a perverted antipathy towards him. But the image remains; it cannot be effaced though it is corrupted by this tragic perversion. Restoration can only be achieved in Christ, 'the image (*eikōn*) of the invisible God' (Col. 1.15) in whom the tragic reversal is itself reversed. 'The whole scriptural witness makes clear that our understanding of the image of God can be sound only when in unbreakable relation to the witness regarding Jesus Christ, who is called the image of God.'[17]

The Christian account of humankind is neither cynically pessimistic nor foolishly optimistic. Because humankind is created by God and sustained by his goodness, it possesses inherent dignity and worth. Despite the tragedy of sin which manifested itself so blatantly in the holocausts and gulags of the twentieth century and seems set to do so again in our present age, men and women remain the bearers of the divine image no matter how inverted it has become. They are capable of experiencing communion with the Creator. They have the potentiality to be redeemed. Yet sin should never be discounted or its effects minimized. Sin is not a superficial blemish which can be ignored or removed by education, culture or moral striving. It is a radical perversion of the soul and an insidious blight which

---

16 Karl Barth, *Church Dogmatics* IV/2, *The Doctrine of Reconciliation* (Edinburgh: T & T Clark, 1958), p. 483.
17 Gerrit C. Berkouwer, *Man: The Image of God* (Grand Rapids: Eerdmans, 1962), p. 107.

riddles the structures of society and rots civilization from within. Its seriousness can be gauged by the fact that it required God's intervention in the person of his Son to free human beings from its tyranny. The doctrine of humanity leads, both logically and theologically, to the doctrines of the person and work of Christ.

Questions for Discussion

1 To what extent are human beings unique in God's creation?

2 How would you best describe the divine image in humankind?

3 'Christianity is not the answer to our ecological problems but their cause.' Why do you think that people make this claim, and is it justified?

4 How can we best explain sin in today's world?

5 Pride and arrogance or self-abasement and self-loathing; which is most sinful?

6 Is there such a thing as 'structural sin' or 'community sin' or should we think of sin as being something which affects only the individual?

6

'The coming of the Exiled King'
The Person of Christ

The Humanity of Christ

In one of his greatest poems, the Quaker Waldo Williams described Jesus Christ as 'the Exiled King'.[1] Although the divine redeemer, he is always fully human, fully one of us.

Throughout the New Testament Jesus Christ is pictured uniformly as having an integrated personality characterized by elements both human and divine. His human nature is patent in that he was descended from normal forebears (Matt. 1.1–6; Luke 3.23–38), that he was born and grew up within an ordinary family (Matt. 1.25; Mark 6.1–6), that he ate, drank, hungered, thirsted and became weary like anyone else (Matt. 21.18; 11.19; John 4.6). He was, in truth, 'like his brothers and sisters in every respect' (Heb. 2.17). These physical aspects of humanness were matched by psychological traits: he was tempted, experienced pain and its implications, loneliness and dejection (Matt. 4.1–11; Mark 14.33–36), he experienced grief at the loss of a friend (John 11.33), anger at unrighteousness (Matt. 21.12–13; John 2.13–22) and trepidation at the prospect of having to face death (Mark 14.33). He was 'one who in every respect has been tested as we are, yet without sin'

---

1 From the poem 'Mewn dau gae' ('Between two fields'), Waldo Williams, *Dail Pren* ('The Leaves of a Tree') (Aberystwyth: Gwasg Aberystwyth, 1956), pp. 15–17, trans. Tony Conran, in *Waldo Williams: The Peacemaker* (Llandysul: Gomer Press, 1997), pp. 132–3.

(Heb. 4.15). Jesus of Nazareth was manifestly a human being among human beings, of the same stuff as the rest of created humanity.

Christ's resurrection from the dead, his transformation from an earthly to a heavenly existence, in no way diminished his human form. The risen Christ and the crucified Christ are one and the same. He bids Thomas, his disciple, to reach out and feel his hands and his side, the *physical* marks of the crucifixion (John 20.27); he assures his followers that he is risen *indeed*:

> He said to them, 'Why are you frightened, and why do doubts arise in your hearts? Look at my hands and my feet; see that it is I myself. Touch me and see; for a ghost does not have flesh and bones as you see I have.' (Luke 24.38–9)

Neither the earthly Jesus nor the risen Christ was a phantom figure. He was fully human both before and after his resurrection from the dead.

Such, too, was the unanimous conviction not only of the Gospel-writers but of the New Testament Epistles as well. Christ came in 'the form of a slave' (Phil. 2.7); he was born 'of a woman' (Gal. 4.4); according to the flesh he was a Jew (Rom. 9.5). In this very human Jesus, God was revealed 'in the flesh' (1 Tim. 3.16). In the risen Christ humanity has been glorified but humanity it remains (1 Cor. 15.12–58). The apostle John in his letters is not only equally insistent upon Christ's true humanity but is openly hostile towards those who would deny it: 'By this you know the Spirit of God: every spirit that confesses that Jesus Christ has come *in the flesh* is from God, and every spirit that does not confess Jesus [in the flesh] is not from God. And this is the spirit of antichrist' (1 John 4.2–3). John's polemic is against those false teachers who would deny the humanity of Christ on the assumption that God cannot involve himself in sinful, finite and mortal humanity. Not so, says the Gospel of John, for 'the Word *became flesh* and lived among us, and we have seen his glory, the glory as of a father's only son, full of grace and truth' (John 1.14). The author of Hebrews, as we have seen, fully concurs with this core Christian conviction:

> Therefore he had to become like his brothers and sisters in every respect, so that he might be a merciful and faithful high priest in the service of God, to make a sacrifice of atonement for the sins of the people. Because he himself was tested by what he suffered, he is able to help those who are being tested. (Heb. 2.17–18)

The humanity of Christ is an actual, a real, an indisputable humanity. It is this humanity, resurrected and glorified and eternally conjoined with his deity, that is essential for our redemption.

> Since, then, we have a great high priest who has passed through the heavens, Jesus, the Son of God, let us hold fast to our confession. For we do not have a high priest who is unable to sympathise with our weaknesses, but we have one who in every respect has been tested as we are, yet without sin. Let us therefore approach the throne of grace with boldness, so that we may receive mercy and find grace to help in time of need. (Heb. 4.14–16)

At the beginning it was not altogether easy for people to accept this truth. For those who had been brought up in the Jewish faith, God was awesome and transcendent; he certainly would not be expected to come among his people in the guise of a wandering rabbi from an obscure country town. When the church broke the bounds of its Jewish environment and began attracting Romans and Greeks, it had to contend with religious preconceptions which held that spirit and flesh could never be combined. For the Greeks, to be spiritual meant to break free from the material realities of the flesh and to strive for the ethereal realm in which the divine was thought to dwell. The idea that God came down from above and took up abode with men and women *as* a man was troubling in the extreme. Such was the strength of feeling against such a conviction that there were those who claimed that Christ only *seemed* to be human; these were the 'docetists' – from the Greek word *dokeō*, to seem – whose ideas were challenged roundly by the apologists and theologians of the early church. According to Ignatius, a colourful Christian leader from Antioch during the first generation after the New Testament:

> For my own part, I know and believe that He was in actual human flesh, even after his resurrection. When He appeared to Peter and his companions, He said to them, 'Take hold of me; touch me, and see that I am no bodiless phantom'. And they touched him then and there, and believed, for they had had contact with the flesh-and-blood reality of him ... After all, if everything our Lord did was only illusion, then these chains of mine must be illusory too! Also, to what end have I given myself up to perish by fire or sword or savage beast?[2]

At the time Ignatius was being transported to Rome to stand trial for refusing to swear allegiance to Trajan, the so-called divine ruler of the empire. He had already suffered for his faith in the flesh. Had Christ merely *appeared* to be human, what point would there be in following him

---

2 Ignatius of Antioch, *The Epistle to the Smyrneans* 3–4, in Andrew Louth (ed.), *Early Christian Writings* (Harmondsworth: Penguin Books, 1987), pp.101–2.

even to death? The reality of the incarnation demanded a much more realistic response than this. Genuine spirituality was not ethereal or flesh-less; it was of the body or it was nothing.

The same was true of Irenaeus (*fl.* 175–95), the influential Bishop of Lyon in Gaul (today's France), and the early church's first systematic theologian. In explaining his idea that Christ, as the second Adam, had undone the sin and disobedience of the first Adam and by so doing restored humankind to fellowship with God, he emphasized the role of the flesh of Christ, Jesus' full and unfeigned unity with the rest of humankind:

> The victory over the enemy [viz. death and the devil] would not have been rightly won had not his conqueror been born as man from a woman. For it was through a woman that the devil held sway over man from the beginning, when he set himself to be man's adversary. Therefore the Lord confesses himself to be the Son of Man, restoring to himself that original man from whom is derived that part of creation which is born of woman.[3]

The North African Christian Tertullian (*c.* 170–*c.* 220), another larger-than-life figure whose contribution to the intellectual life of the early church was enormous, turned all his rhetorical skills – and his withering sarcasm – against those who believed that Christ's full and real humanity had only been a sham:

> Was not God really crucified? Did he not really die after a real crucifixion? Did he not really rise again, after real

3 Irenaeus, *Against the Heretics* 5 xx 2, in Henry Bettenson (ed.), *The Early Christian Fathers*, 4th edn (Oxford: Oxford University Press, 1978), p. 82.

death? ... If the flesh with its sufferings was a figment, then the Spirit with its mighty works was unreal. Why do you cut Christ in half with a lie?[4]

Patently, there was something of profound importance at stake in these claims. Had Christ been anything less than fully human, where would that have left the human race? The answer, of course: forsaken by God and perpetually alienated from him. Alternatively, the fact that Christ was (and remains) fully human lends dignity, meaning and worth to *all* our human activities. All spiritualities, whether ancient or modern, which downgrade the flesh are to be rejected outright. 'This Docetism,' says Berkouwer, 'as history has clearly shown, is a matter of life or death for the church. Every doctrine teaching "a divine Christ" who has nothing to do with the genuinely human is a threat to the faith.'[5]

The Deity of Christ

Despite this conviction concerning the full humanity of Christ, the church, on the basis of scripture, has always held fast to the reality of his divinity as well. We need not say any more about this than was noted above, in Chapter 4. In Christ's human flesh God was specifically present. God was in Christ not only in the sense of merely inspiring him as God could be said to inspire all Spirit-filled men or women, but God was so indissolubly conjoined with humanity in Jesus' person that Christ was God incarnate. The Gospels portray a man who possessed a unique sense

---

4 Tertullian, *Of the Flesh of Christ* 4–5, in Bettenson (ed.), *The Early Christian Fathers*, pp. 125–6.
5 Gerrit C. Berkouwer, *The Person of Christ* (Grand Rapids: Eerdmans, 1954), p. 227.

of unity with the Father and who claimed a moral authority over all people. He claimed to speak with God's own authority making commitment to him synonymous with commitment to God. He claimed for himself the power to forgive sins – a quite staggering assertion considering the character of Jewish religion and its belief in the one true God above – and assumed the prerogative to pronounce the final judgement on humankind. These claims were presented in the context of a life of spotless integrity and manifest humility, and led the early Christians to one conclusion: that this man Jesus was, in fact, divine. 'In him all the fullness of God was pleased to dwell' (Col. 1.19). He was none other than God incarnate, God having been made flesh, God personally present and active for the redemption of humankind.

The Unity of Christ's Person

The twin aspects of Christ's person, his humanity and his deity and the nature of their interrelation, became the objects for special attention during the fourth and fifth centuries AD. It was then that the church formulated (in a way that has become normative for all subsequent believers) its Christology, that is its doctrine concerning the person of Christ. The councils of the church which had met at Nicaea, a city in what is now north-west Turkey, in AD 325 and at Constantinople in AD 381 had already formulated the doctrine of the Trinity and pronounced Christ as being 'of the same substance (*homoousios*) with the Father'. His deity, therefore, was affirmed. The problem which remained was how best to reconcile that deity with his humanity within a single person. The christological development which led to the famous definition on the person of Christ made at the Council of Chalcedon in AD 451, occurred like this:

Alexandrian and Antiocene thought

The theologians of the Christian city of Alexandria in Egypt were, in the main, Platonists. For them the universal was more important than the particular, that is 'humanity' as an abstract concept rather than the men and women who embodied it. But more significant than their philosophical assumptions were their convictions concerning the absolute pre-eminence of God in revelation and redemption. When they reflected on Christ they saw, embodied in him, the divine Logos pre-eminent; for them Jesus of Nazareth was, first and foremost, not a Jewish rabbi who had taught men and women about the Father, but the divine Word who had taken human form. Their favourite text was John 1.14, 'And the Word became flesh and lived among us'. Although the Alexandrine emphasis never denied the full and proper humanity of Jesus, nevertheless it majored on his deity, that Christ was *God* having become human.

The theologians of Antioch, another important Christian centre in the Middle East, were, in the main, Aristotelians. For them the particular was more important than the general. In Antioch, universal concepts were merely a convenient way of classifying similar or different groups of objects. So whereas the Alexandrines emphasized the divinity of Christ, that Jesus was the divine Logos having been made flesh – both *Logos* and *flesh* are abstract terms – for the theologians of Antioch the more concrete humanity of Christ was the first thing that they considered. For them the human nature of Christ was more than an appendage to his divinity, rather it was the essential starting point for a correct understanding of his person. So if the Alexandrines tended towards monism, giving prominence to the divine Logos in Christ, the Antiochenes tended towards dualism with the human nature of Christ being regarded separately from his divinity. Their favourite texts were from the birth narratives in Matthew and Luke, which depicted a very human saviour having been born to Mary, or else Paul's less abstract idea in the Philippians of Jesus having 'taken the form of a slave ... and being found in human form' (Phil. 2.7). This Christ, though conjoined with the rest of created humanity, was, nevertheless, a particular, distinct, individual human being and not just an abstraction which served as the vehicle for the divine Word. Their whole emphasis was on the co-presence of two simultaneous natures in Christ and not merely on the divine with the human in subordination to it. 'While not denying the involvement of God the Logos in the incarnate life', the Antiochene tradition, notes H. E. W. Turner, 'was chiefly concerned to produce adequate living space for the humanity of Christ which was more highly valued and more realistically conceived than in the rival tradition.'[6]

Apollinaris (c. 310–90)

So far it was a matter of emphasis, two different traditions within a broader Christian consensus. The danger was for these different emphases to be pushed too far thus endangering on the one hand Christ's human nature or his divine nature on the other. The history of the christological controversy is how these dangers were faced and eventually, at Chalcedon in AD 451, overcome.

Apollinaris was Bishop of Laodicea in Syria and a colleague of Athanasius, the great champion of Christ's divinity and of his being 'of the same substance (*homoousios*) with the Father'. Typical of his fellow Alexandrines, Apollinaris stressed the divine pre-eminence of Christ, God's unique Logos or Word. For him the Logos had descended into human life, it had interrupted or broken into human-

---

6 H. E. W. Turner, *Jesus the Christ* (Oxford: Mowbray, 1976), p. 38.

ity. So keen was he to emphasize this divine involvement in humanity through Christ that he virtually did away with Christ's human side. 'There is but one Christ, and he is divine' was his claim. The person of Christ, for Apollinaris, was Logos-centred; his humanity was merely incidental, lacking in any independent value or significance. In other words, he took the Alexandrine emphasis to extremes; he so stressed Christ's divinity as virtually to exclude his humanity. Instead of possessing a human mind or soul, which was conjoined to the divine nature, the divine Logos, stated Apollinaris, had displaced the human soul.

The church knew instinctively that such an idea was wrong. It was in conflict with the Gospels' picture of Christ as having complete humanity and was injurious to the doctrine of salvation. How could humankind be saved without God having himself become human? As Gregory of Nazianzus had said: 'If God did not assume human nature, he cannot redeem human kind.' So this was the first round in the christological controversy. The church knew that an adequate doctrine of incarnation would have to give due emphasis to Christ's human nature. Apollinaris' mistake was to have alerted it to the fact: 'The strength of Apollinaris lies in his firm grasp of the divine involvement in incarnation. His fatal weakness lay in his defective sense of the place of the humanity both in christology and redemption.'[7]

Nestorius (d. 451)

If Apollinaris belonged to the school of Alexandria, Nestorius' thought was Aniochene. A pupil of the foremost of Antioch's theologians, Theodore of Mopsuestia, Nestorius had a high doctrine of humanity. Humankind was

---

7 Turner, *Jesus the Christ*, p. 42.

the crown of God's good creation and as such possessed unique dignity. It followed that the humanity of Christ, his human nature as contrasted with the divine, should never be allowed to be demoted or eclipsed by the divine Logos. To stress the Logos' invasion of the flesh as it were, would be to denigrate the reality of Christ. The redemption of humankind was only achieved by the victory of the *man* Jesus Christ over sin and death. It was not that the divine Logos so over-ruled the human will that it was not possible for Christ to disobey the divine will (*non posse peccare*), but that Christ was indeed free, in fact and in theory, to fall yet he used his human will to overcome the possibility of disobedience and sin (*posse non peccare*). In Christ, human as well as divine, perfect freedom had been exercised thus fulfilling God's intentions for humankind. And for Christ to triumph over sin as a human being, it was of paramount importance that he had a human soul. Whatever the divine involvement in the incarnation was, Christ's full humanity must not be jeopardized.

Nestorius postulated a threefold division in human nature: the *ousia* (essence) or general humanity, that which joins a man or a woman to humanity as such; the *phusis* (nature) being the way in which that general humanity manifests itself in an individual person; and the *prosōpon* (literally, 'face'), how those individual characteristics rise to the surface in the way a man or woman lives their life and appears to their fellows. As Christ was fully human, sharing in all of humankind's attributes, he too shared in this psychological make-up. His person was indeed fully unified and integrated, the divine being in complete psychological conjunction with the human. However, for Nestorius, this integration was only fully operative on the third level, that of the *prosōpon*, surface level as it were. For Nestorius Christ had *two* essences (*ousia*), the one being in solidarity with God the Father and the other with humankind; he had *two* sets of attributes or natures (*phusis*), the one befitting his godhead and the other his humanity; and, third, he had only one *prosōpon*, the level on which the human and the divine came together as an integrated whole. 'The two natures', he claimed, 'were united by their union in a single *prosōpon*.'[8]

Whatever else Nestorius was guilty of, he cannot be blamed for holding personally to the theory of a schizoid Christ. He believed in a unified, fully human and fully divine saviour. Yet by defining that union on such a superficial level he left himself open to the charge of christological schizophrenia, that the one Christ was really two beings trapped within a single entity: 'This was a travesty of what Nestorius intended to teach, but he had only his own failure to tackle the problem of the Lord's Person at a deeper level to blame.'[9] As H. E. W. Turner states: 'The heresy of Nestorius lay not in an explicit affirmation of a double personality in Christ but in his failure to give a convincing account of the unity of Christ in which he evidently believed.'[10]

Eutyches (c.378–454)

The third milestone on the road to Chalcedon was marked by the theories of 'the aged and muddle-headed archiamandrite' Eutyches, 'the founder of an extreme and virtually docetic form of monophysitism, teaching the Lord's humanity was totally absorbed by his divinity'.[11] (An archiamandrite is a functionary in the Eastern Church, while monophysitism is the belief that Christ possessed only one

---

8 J. N. D. Kelly, *Early Christian Doctrines*, 5th edn (London: A & C Black, 1978), p. 315.

9 Kelly, *Early Christian Doctrines*, p. 317.

10 Turner, *Jesus the Christ*, p. 51.

11 Kelly, *Early Christian Doctrines*, p. 331.

(*mono*) nature (*phusis*)). Unlike Apollinaris and Nestorius he was neither a serious theologian nor a profound thinker, yet his views were sufficiently influential to merit specific condemnation at the Council of Chalcedon.

According to Eutyches, Christ's divine nature remains the same while, at the point of incarnation, his human nature was extinguished. There occurred something akin to a chemical reaction whereby the dual natures of Christ were made into a single, transformed divine substance. The union of the two natures occurred in the Virgin's womb. Thereafter Christ possessed a single, non-human, divine being: 'After the union I confess one nature.' Although these views retained a certain popularity among Christians during the early fifth century, there was no doubt that they would be rejected ultimately. According to Leo the Great, leader of the Western Church, in his *Tome* or doctrinal letter of AD 431:

> Eutuches did not realize ... [that] Jesus Christ ... is true God and also true man. There is no unreality in this unity ... for just as the God is not changed by his compassion, so the man is not swallowed up by the Godhead.[12]

Such was the doctrinal background of the Chalcedonian definition.

The Chalcedonian Definition

Nestorius' theory had been condemned as heretical by a council of the church that met at Ephesus in AD 431, but Eutychianism retained popularity (despite Leo the Great and despite its inherent improbabilities) for a long time to come. However, the orthodox Christian emperor Marcian

---

12 Leo the Great, *Letter to Flavian* 2–4, in Bettenson (ed.), *The Early Christian Fathers*, pp. 278–80,

realized the gravity of the issues and called the bishops and other leaders of the church together for a further council, at Chalcedon over the Bospherous from his capital in Constantinople, in AD 451. Here 520 bishops attended, all of whom were from the Eastern Church though Leo, Bishop of Rome and leader of the Western Church (who could not be there personally), was represented by four deputies. The whole church already held to God's trinitarian nature as defined by the Nicene Creed in AD 325 and AD 381. Now the delegates proceeded to define the boundaries of the community's understanding of Christ's person. This would be based on Leo's *Tome* or doctrinal letter and some of the letters of Cyril, the patriarch of Alexandria. Thus there was a universal input – Rome, Alexandria, Antioch and Constantinople – into the council's proceedings. 'Whatever else may be said for or against Chalcedon,' says John Macquarrie, 'its pronouncements must be reckoned one of the most truly ecumenical in the entire history of the church.'[13]

> We all with one voice confess our Lord Jesus Christ one and the same Son, truly God and truly human, the same consisting of a reasonable soul and a body, of one substance with the Father as touching the Godhead, the same of one substance with us as touching the humanity ... to be acknowledged in two natures, without confusion, without change, without division, without separation.[14]

The definition may be summarized simply as Christ being 'truly God, truly human and truly one'. He existed in two

---

13 John Macquarrie in Cyril S. Rodd (ed.), *Foundation Documents of the Faith* (Edinburgh: T & T Clark, 1987), p. 71.
14 J. Stevenson (ed.), *Creeds, Councils and Controversies: Documents Illustrative of the History of the Church AD 337–461* (London: SPCK, 1966), p. 337, translation revised.

natures, human and divine. The human was completely ours, except for sin. The divine nature was the same as God the Father. But the two were united in a single person without being separated or mixed: 'without confusion, without change, without division, without separation'. Thus the theories of Apollinaris, Nestorius and Eutyches were each rejected. 'For the majority it was, and has remained, a normative statement guiding the church in all her subsequent attempts to understand more fully the Person of Christ.'[15] It was more a guide to understanding than a definitive understanding itself. The definition never presumed to provide any explanations of *how* the human could be conjoined with the divine; this remained, and remains, a mystery: 'Who knows how God is made flesh and yet remains God? This only faith understands, adoring the Logos in silence.'[16] What the Chalcedonian definition does is to assert what the faith demands on the basis of the New Testament evidence of who Christ was and what his life, death and obedience achieved. It was, and remains, normative for the Christian church: 'It sets out to provide the limits within which the task, if it is to be attempted at all, must be done.'[17] The mystery of Christ, therefore, as confessed by the church, consists of two natures, the one fully divine and the other fully human, in perfect unity, harmony and integration. This was *the* consequence of Chalcedon.

The question, of course, is: where does that leave us today? It may be that the deliberations of Christian fathers long ago seem remote from the spiritual concerns of the twenty-first century, but the truth of the Chalcedon defin-

---

15 Maurice Wiles, *The Early Christian Fathers* (London: SCM Press, 1975), p. 80.
16 Maximus the Confessor, *Ambigua* 5, quoted by William C. Placher, *Jesus the Savior: The Meaning of Jesus Christ for Christian Faith* (Louisville: Westminster John Knox Press, 2001), p. 206.
17 Wiles, *The Early Christian Fathers*, p. 80.

ition, that Jesus Christ is 'truly God, truly human and truly one', is of abiding importance for us all. It says something of timeless significance about God, humankind and about our relation with him. The contemporary US theologian William C. Placher has made the point well: that our sin had so cut us off from God that, before anything else could happen, God had to re-establish contact, and that meant changing wayward, lost, sinful humanity into something open to connection with God.

> The incarnation re-established that contact in the most dramatic way imaginable. When the Word became flesh, what it means to be human changed for each of us – you, me, Hitler, the bag lady, and the heroin addict huddled on a street corner on a winter night – because in one human being humanity was united with divinity. 'For you know the generous act of our Lord Jesus Christ, that though he was rich, yet for your sakes he became poor, so that by his poverty you might become rich' (2 Cor. 8.9) ... In the incarnation of the divine Word ... humanity is transformed – not just for Jesus but for all of us. It has become a different thing to be a human being.[18]

We should give the theologians of Chalcedon credit for making this truth a possibility and a reality for us all.

Questions for Discussion

1 What is the scriptural evidence for Christ's full humanity?

2 Who were the Docetists? Why were they uncomfortable with the idea that Christ was fully human?

---

18 Placher, *Jesus the Savior*, pp. 46–7, 50.

3 What was the main weakness of (a) Apollinarius'
   understanding, and (b) Nestorius' understanding of
   the person of Christ? Do their ideas have parallels
   today?

4 Why do we need creeds? Are they a help or a hindrance
   to our current knowledge of Jesus Christ?

5 Is it possible to believe that Jesus is both human *and*
   divine?

6 Is it *necessary* to believe that Jesus is both human and
   divine, and if so, why?

7

'The reconciling exchange'
The Work of Christ

Incarnation and Atonement

We have already seen that Jesus Christ is both human and
divine as well as being fully one person. As a human being
he was uniquely responsive to God's call and wholly obedient to the Father's will in all things. As the Logos of God,
on the other hand, he was God at work among us, restoring
a marred creation and inaugurating the promised kingdom
within our world. But he was not two beings but one, the
fully integrated God-man whose person was at all times
and under all circumstances both human and divine 'without confusion, without change, without division, without
separation'. Both aspects of this person should be given
equal prominence: not Christ's humanity to the detriment
of his deity (as it tended to be among the theologians of
Antioch), or Christ's deity to the detriment of his humanity
(as the tendency was among the Christians of Alexandria).
Christ is both the sovereign Lord who became flesh, the
Son of God who exercised God's dominion – and, paradoxically, his humility – in the healing of creation and the
forgiveness of sins, and at the same time the humble and
suffering servant, the Son of man, wholly obedient to the
Father's will who fulfilled our covenant obligations towards God to the letter. Jesus Christ, therefore, was God
among humankind and a human being wholly obedient,

sensitive and responsive to God. Both aspects of Christ's person would become essential for a sound comprehension of the nature of Christ's work.

Christ's active sacrificial obedience culminated in his death on the cross. Some interpretations of the doctrine of the atonement have so emphasized Christ's death that they have minimized the significance of his perpetually obedient response to God's will during his mission and life. His death has been understood in terms of an external transaction between the Father and the Son which occurred on the cross. On Calvary Christ endured a penal judgement apart from us and in our place where he was 'smitten by the Father's rod' in order to assuage the divine anger or else to fulfil the inexorable penalty which we had accrued because we had broken the divine law. Such a theory pits the Father against the Son and undermines the basic evangelical truth that it is *God* who loves us and he does so *unconditionally*: 'For *God* so loved the world that he *gave* his only Son' (John 3.16a). Christ did not have to turn God's wrath into mercy on the condition of sacrificing himself; God (who was none other than the God who was eternally one with Jesus Christ and the Holy Spirit) was *already* merciful towards humankind. It was John Calvin who said, rightly: 'It was not after we were reconciled to him through the blood of his Son that he began to love us. Rather, he has loved us before the world was created.'[1] It may well be that God judged human sinfulness and that Christ, who was God, stepped into the place where that sinfulness was judged, annihilated and done away with for good; what the Father did *not* do was to punish the Son in order to be merciful to humankind or in order to forgive men and women their sins. An external, forensic or legal concept of Christ's work that divorces his atoning death from the whole process of

---

1 John Calvin, *Institutes of the Christian Religion* 2.16.4 (Philadelphia: Westminster Press, 1960), p. 506.

his sacrificial life does scant justice to the New Testament evidence or to the loving character of the biblical God. It implies a rift between God the Father and God the Son and drives a sharp wedge between the incarnation and the atonement. A sound atonement doctrine needs to be rooted not only in what Christ did but in who Christ was, otherwise it would be apart from us and over our heads. We are not the involuntary beneficiaries of a legal transaction in which we have no part, but by partaking of the life which Christ came among us to share, the atonement becomes as intimately relevant to us as the fact that we have been created by God and in God's image, and that God having taken flesh, *our* flesh, links us to the depths of Christ's very being.

In order to prevent Christ's atoning death from being divorced from his sacrificial life, a radical doctrine of incarnation is essential. We need to hold to a *real* incarnation, the idea that God, in assuming flesh, assumed real, alienated, fallen, even sinful flesh, and he did this in order to effect a real atonement between God and an alienated, fallen and sinful humanity. It was axiomatic for early Christian theology that 'what was not assumed was not healed'.[2] In order to be saved, redeemed or made whole, human nature *as it was*, in its very corruption and sinful rebellion against God, needed to be taken up by God so that it could be purified and cleansed. So much traditional theology, both Catholic and Protestant, has assumed that God, in becoming human, took upon himself either *perfect* human nature, like Adam's before the fall, or else some sort of *neutral* human nature unblemished by sin and unaffected by human imperfection. Somehow God should not be allowed to sully himself by becoming involved with

2 E.g. Gregory of Nazianzus, *Epistle* 101.7, in Henry Bettenson (ed.), *The Early Christian Fathers*, 4th edn (Oxford: Oxford University Press, 1978), p. 108.

human beings as they are, under the judgement of sin and in their abject corruption. But this is not what the gospel is about and certainly this is not what the New Testament teaches:

> For God has done what the law, weakened by the flesh, could not do: by sending his own Son in the likeness of sinful flesh (*en homoiōmati sarkos hamartias*), and to deal with sin, he condemned sin in the flesh, so that the just requirement of the law might be fulfilled in us, who walk not according to the flesh but according to the Spirit. (Rom. 8.3–4)

In other words, God involved himself not in human perfection but in human imperfection; the curse which he took upon himself was our curse: 'Christ redeemed us from the curse of the law *by becoming a curse for us* ... so that we might receive the promise of the Spirit through faith' (Gal. 3.14–15). Adam before the fall was *not* cursed or under judgement, neither does neutral or unblemished human nature need to be redeemed. What happened in Christ was altogether more radical than a timid theology would allow us to believe. In the mystery of the incarnation God came into the depths of human antipathy to God, humankind's radical conflict with God and a human nature which was corrupt to the core. Christ *became sin* on our behalf: 'For our sake he made him *to be sin* who knew no sin, so that in him we might become the righteousness of God' (2 Cor. 5.21). This does not mean that Christ himself was corrupt or that he was affected by the sinfulness from which he came to redeem us. As the New Testament makes abundantly clear, he was, in fact, wholly without sin. Through the Spirit, from birth to death, Christ in his humanity lived a life in perfect harmony with God as God's covenant partner and by so doing he began to heal, redeem and sanctify the flesh that he, through the divine condescension, had chosen to share. In the very act of taking our real human nature upon himself, Christ's wholeness, sanctity and perfection were at work actively on our behalf. In other words, God in Christ was not one remove from humanity but intimately involved in our humanity by living a perfect human life, and in the Spirit he overcame the estrangement, sin, guilt and death which had entrenched itself in our humanity and a life which culminated in death. The incarnation and the atonement are so intimately bound together that Christ lived a vicarious life from the very beginning whereby costly human obedience and the divine approval came together as one. In a very deep sense, Christ himself, and not just that which he achieved, *is* the atonement between ourselves and God: 'He is the atoning sacrifice for our sins, and not for ours only but for the sins of the whole world' (1 John 2.2).

If this is the case, that our redemption is made good not by Christ's death alone but by Christ's whole incarnate life which culminated in death, why does the New Testament put such an inordinate emphasis on the cross? After all it was the apostle Paul who wrote: 'We were reconciled to God *through the death of his Son* ... through whom we have now received the atonement' (Rom. 5.10–11, RSV). The answer to this must be in the way in which Jesus of Nazareth himself interpreted his impending fate at the hands of the authorities: 'Then he began to teach them that the Son of Man must undergo great suffering, and be rejected by the elders, the chief priests, and the scribes, and be killed, and after three days rise again' (Mark 8.31; cf. Matt. 16.21; Luke 9.22). It was only after Peter had made his confession that Christ was the Messiah that Jesus turned his back on Galilee where he had been received as a popular preacher, rabbi and healer, and made his way, ominously, towards Jerusalem. Thereafter he struck this sombre note again:

'For the Son of Man came not to be served but to serve, and to give his life a ransom for many' (Mark 10.45; cf. Matt. 20.28). Now that he was in Jerusalem, in the company of his disciples at the feast of the Passover, the expectation of his own death provided the context and meaning for the Lord's Supper:

> When they were eating, he took a loaf of bread, and after blessing it he broke it, gave it to them, and said, 'Take; this is my body.' Then he took a cup, and after giving thanks he gave it to them, and all of them drank from it. He said to them, 'This is my blood of the covenant, which is poured out for many.' (Mark 14.22–24; cf. Matt. 26.26–29; cf. Luke 22.14–23)

The symbolic background for these momentous words and sacred actions was unmistakable: the Old Testament scriptures that linked the coming messianic rule with innocent suffering and the blood of the covenant:[3] 'Moses took the blood and dashed it on the people, and said, "See the blood of the covenant that the LORD has made with you in accordance with all these words"' (Exod. 24.8).

> But he was wounded for our transgressions,
>   crushed for our iniquities;
> upon him was the punishment that made us whole,
>   and by his bruises we are healed ...
> and the LORD has laid on him
>   the iniquity of us all. (Isa. 53.5–6)

What is apparent here is that Christ offered up his life as a sacrifice, propitiation or ransom which would effect the redemption of humankind:

> Jesus declares that he has come as the servant to medi-

---

3 cf. Exod. 24.3–8; Isa. 42.6–7; 49.8; 53.1–12; Jer. 31.31–4 etc.

ate God's covenant with his people and offer his life in an act of sacrifice that will emancipate the lives of many (i.e. of all, as St Paul interpreted it). It was his whole life, and above all that life poured out in the supreme sacrifice of death on the Cross, that made atonement for sin, and constituted the price of redemption for mankind.[4]

Thereafter the message, preaching and faith of the apostolic church had to do with 'Christ, and him crucified' (1 Cor. 2.2b). It was the cross that became the symbol of God's free, unstinting grace which was such an affront to human pride and such a condemnation of our sin and wilful rebellion against him. It was through the cross (not apart from Christ's perfect life but following on from his costly, arduous, lifelong obedience) that the ransom was paid, that expiation was made for our sins, that our old nature was judged, displaced and destroyed, that God's holy righteousness triumphed and that we were reconciled with him: 'In Christ God was reconciling the world to himself, not counting their trespasses against them' (2 Cor. 5.19). If there is an element of penal substitution in the atonement – that Christ substituted himself for us in order to pay the price for our redemption – it is not apart from us or over our heads, as it were, but it is one in which we are deeply involved as those for whom he came to share and purify our sinladen humanity.

Sacrifice, Reconciliation and Redemption

The principal element that brings together the range of Old Testament references through which Jesus, and the early church, interpreted his passion and death is that of

4 Thomas F. Torrance, *The Trinitarian Faith: The Evangelical Theology of the Ancient Catholic Church* (Edinburgh: T & T Clark, 1988), p. 169.

sacrifice. It was as a perfect sacrifice to God the Father that Jesus the Son offered his life.

The range of Old Testament sacrifices included communion-sacrifices as illustrated by the rituals in Leviticus 3 and 7 whereby food was dedicated to God and those who partook of it were deemed to have shared in a sacred meal in his presence. Another category was that of sacrifices of praise and thanksgiving including the burnt offerings of Leviticus 1. Since men and women owed everything to their creator and Lord, it was thought fitting to pay tribute to him, and tribute meant giving up something vital from a man's herds or flocks, from his crops or later from his money, in order that God might be honoured. A third category, and one which had come to dominate Israel's temple rituals in Jesus' time, was sacrificial sin-offerings: 'Every day you shall offer a bull as a sin offering for atonement' (Exod. 9.36a; cf. Lev. 4–7). Israel knew that its God was holy and that they, its people, had a legacy of unfaithfulness where the covenant had been transgressed and they had fallen into sin. In order to purge themselves from these sins, an atonement was needed so that their purity could be maintained. They also knew that God was merciful, faithful and forgiving, and that God himself had provided an atonement through the sacrificial blood. The logic of the sin-offerings has been explained by Frances Young:

> The sin-offerings were not human attempts to buy off the anger of the righteous and vindictive God; they were not propitiatory, in the sense that they were an attempt to change God. Rather they were a means given by God himself for wiping away the sins that prevented his chosen people from fulfilling the obligations of the covenant-relationship and offering him fitting worship.[5]

---

5 Frances Young, *Sacrifice and the Death of Christ* (London: SPCK, 1975), p. 28.

Why this should have been achieved by the shedding of blood is never explained. Perhaps the nearest that scripture comes to offering a rationale for blood sacrifice is in the Book of Leviticus: 'For the life of the flesh is in the blood; and I have given it to you for making atonement for your lives on the altar; for, as life, it is the blood that makes atonement' (Lev. 17.11). What we do know is that blood sacrifice is a very potent cultic symbol in many religions and that Israel, and the church, took it as their own.

Along with this cluster of sacrificial motifs, there were two dramatic rituals which rooted the Hebrew people in their history of redemption and reminded them of their covenant responsibility to God: the Feast of the Passover (which has already been mentioned in the context of the Lord's Supper) and the annual Day of Atonement. The original 'passover' had occurred during the exodus from Egypt when God commanded Moses that each household should slaughter a lamb, smear its blood on the door-posts of the house, roast it and eat it with unleavened bread and bitter herbs. When the angel of death came by to kill the firstborn from among the Egyptians, those who sheltered behind the symbol of the blood would be saved (Exod. 12). This story became formative for the Jews (and even more formative for the early Christians) who celebrated through it God's mighty action in redeeming them from their enemies.

The Day of Atonement, which like the Passover was observed annually, was the great culmination of all sin-offerings. This was the only time in the year that the high priest, having confessed the sins of the people and having laid his hands on the sacrificial lamb, entered the most sacred part of the Jerusalem temple, the 'holy of holies', and there, on the 'mercy-seat', the cover of the ark of the covenant, he would sprinkle the animal's blood. James Torrance, who has done so much to remind the church of

the significance of Christ's *human* nature for our understanding of atonement, has described the practice thus:

> In leading Israel's worship the High Priest was the Repre-
> sentative of the people. This was symbolized by the fact
> that he bore the names of the twelve tribes inscribed on
> his breastplate and in the onyx stones on his shoulders.
> All that he did, he did in virtue of his solidarity with
> Israel. The significance of this comes out most clearly
> on the Day of Atonement when the High Priest takes the
> blood of the sacrificial victim and enters within the veil
> into the Holy of Holies and sprinkles the blood on the
> mercy seat. There he intercedes with God for the people,
> and then he returns to the people from God to pronounce
> the Aaronic blessing of peace.[6]

This is the legacy into which Jesus Christ entered. The com-
munion-sacrifice prefigured the Eucharist or Lord's Supper
which was also understood in terms of a renewed Passover
meal – none of these symbols are mutually exclusive – with
Christ himself as the sacrificial lamb; in the words of John
the Baptist: 'Here is the Lamb of God who takes away the
sins of the world' (John 1.29). The apostle Paul maintained
that Christ 'our paschal lamb ... has been sacrificed' (1 Cor.
5.7b) and by so doing brought together elements of the
praise-offering, the sin-offering and the Day of Atonement,
while the lamb motif became the dominant metaphor in
the faith of the persecuted Christians during the time of the
Book or Revelation:

---

6 James B. Torrance in T. H. L. Parker (ed.), *Essays in Christology for
Karl Barth* (London: Lutterworth Press, 1956), pp. 169–70; cf. James B.
Torrance, *Worship, Community and the Triune God of Grace* (Carlisle:
Paternoster Press, 1996), pp. 36–7.

'You are worthy to take the scroll and to open the seals,
   for you were slaughtered and by your blood you
      ransomed for God
   saints from every tribe and language and people and
      nation ...'
'Worthy is the Lamb that was slaughtered
to receive power and wealth and wisdom and might
and honour and glory and blessing! (Rev. 5.9–10, 11b)

Along with the Book of Revelation, it is in the Letter to the Hebrews that these ideas are most graphically expressed, and the twin facts of Christ's lifelong obedience to God as his covenant partner (and the implications of that for our own infirmity as bruised and broken human beings) and his costly sacrifice for our sins, come together in a uniquely evocative way: 'Indeed, under the law almost everything is purified with blood, and without the shedding of blood there is no forgiveness of sins' (Heb. 9.22). Here Christ is both high priest and sacrificial lamb, the victor becomes the victim, and through this costly victory we are reconciled to God:

> Since, then, we have a great high priest who has passed through the heavens, Jesus, the Son of God, let us hold fast to our confession. For we do not have a high priest who is unable to sympathize with our weaknesses, but we have one who in every respect has been tested as we are, yet without sin. Let us therefore approach the throne of grace with boldness, so that we may receive mercy and find grace to help in time of need. (Heb. 4.14–16; cf. 2.17–18)

The main points are summed up in the words of William Placher: 'In sacrificial rituals, people enacted a drama that often involved slaying a victim, and then God would expiate their sins. In Christ, it is God who enacts the drama of expiation and becomes the victim.'[7]

The idea of sacrifice is paralleled by the concepts of reconciliation and redemption. It was the apostle Paul who insisted that it was 'God, who reconciled us to himself through Christ', and has given us in turn 'the ministry of reconciliation; that is, in Christ God was reconciling the world to himself, not counting their trespasses against them, and entrusting the message of reconciliation to us' (2 Cor. 5.18–19). The dominant picture here is one of the healing of a broken relationship or the mending of a fractured friendship; because the language is personal, rather than sacrificial or legal, it chimes in well with our human sensibilities and with our convictions concerning the loving personhood of God. Yet we should remember that reconciliation does not come cheap. It is sin which has caused the rift between ourselves and God and the inevitable response of the holy God to that sin is wrath: 'For the wrath of God is revealed from heaven against *all* ungodliness' (Rom. 1.18a). This is not a matter of divine petulance or of God, as it were, losing his temper. 'The wrath of God is the righteousness of God', wrote the young Karl Barth, 'apart from and without Christ.'[8] The wrath or 'anger' of God is God's unalloyed response to human sinfulness; it implies judgement and destruction. Yet it is never operative (with due respect to Barth) apart from or without Christ. In fact it is in Christ that it is both revealed for what it is and effectively done away with for our redemption: 'For if God himself became man, *this* man, what else can this mean ... [but] that he made *himself* the object of the wrath

---

7 William C. Placher, *Jesus the Savior: The Meaning of Jesus Christ for Christian Faith* (Louisville: Westminster John Knox Press, 2001), p. 134.

8 Karl Barth, *The Epistle to the Romans*, 6th edn (Oxford: Oxford University Press, [1921] 1968), p. 43.

and judgement to which man had brought himself ... *This is how God loved the world*.'[9] This, it seems to me, is the only way we can begin to understand the cry of dereliction from the cross: 'My God, my God, why have you forsaken me?' (Matt. 27.46b). God's holy wrath has been dealt with not by being ignored, trivialized or depersonalized, but by being taken up into the triune God himself on the cross. It was through Christ that 'God was pleased to reconcile to himself all things, whether in earth or in heaven, by making peace through the blood of his cross' (Col. 1.20).

The other chief term which is used in connection with Christ's sacrificial work on the cross is redemption. Redemption means, literally, 'to buy back'. In the biblical world it denoted the action of one's kin to recover the forfeited property of a family member (Lev. 25.25; Ruth 4.4–6), or else the action of purchasing the freedom of a family member who had fallen into slavery. The one who did the purchasing was the 'redeemer'. It did not take long for the Hebrew people to see themselves as the ones who had been bought back or 'redeemed', not by a member of the family but by the great and merciful covenant God himself: 'Our Redeemer – the LORD of hosts is his name – is the Holy One of Israel' (Isa. 47.4). Just as God had saved them from their enemies during the exodus from Egypt at the beginning of the Old Testament, during their exile in Babylon towards the end of the Old Testament they had faith that God would deliver them again: 'For the LORD has ransomed Israel and has redeemed him from hands too strong for him' (Jer. 31.11). God here was seen to act on Israel's behalf in virtue of his covenant relationship with his people.

How was it that this idea came to be Christianized? It was simple enough: 'You know that you were ransomed from the futile ways inherited from your ancestors, not

---

9 Karl Barth, *Church Dogmatics* II/2, *The Doctrine of God* (Edinburgh: T & T Clark, 1957), pp. 164, 165, emphases added.

with perishable things like silver or gold, but with the precious blood of Christ, like that of a lamb without defect or blemish' (1 Pet. 1.18–19). Here the sacrificial motif was woven together with the redemptory ideal and actualized in Christ. It was 'Christ Jesus, himself human, who gave himself a ransom for all' (1 Tim. 2.5b–6). The idea of being set free for a price – 'you are not your own, for you were bought with a price, therefore glorify God in your body' (1 Cor. 6.19b–20) – was linked by the early Christians with the idea of being released by Christ from slavery and bondage as though the people were the spoils of war: 'He disarmed the rulers and authorities, and made a public example of them, triumphing over them in [the cross]' (Col. 2.15). These 'rulers and authorities' were not so much earthly powers as mighty spiritual foes: 'For our struggle is not against enemies of blood and flesh, but against the rulers, against the authorities, against the cosmic powers of this present darkness, against the spiritual forces of evil in the heavenly places' (Eph. 6.12). It is hardly fashionable to talk about the devil even in an invitation to Christian doctrine, neither do we want to give him more than his due. 'If we believe too much in the strength of the devil', wrote Karl Barth, 'we bury Christ again after his resurrection.'[10] Yet there are malignancies in the world that seem greater than the sum of even their most evil parts: the irrational absurdity of sin in which evil seems to take on a force and a personality of its own. 'One of the things that surprised me when I first read the New Testament seriously', wrote C. S. Lewis, 'was that it talked so much about a Dark Power in the universe – a mighty evil spirit who was held to be the Power behind death and disease, and sin.'[11] This 'dark

---

10 Karl Barth, *The Faith of the Church: A Commentary on the Apostles' Creed* (London: Fontana Books, 1960), p. 44.
11 C. S. Lewis, *Mere Christianity* (London: Fontana Books, 1971), p. 47.

power', God's opponent – though never God's equal and the one who is pictured in the gospel narrative as having tempted Christ in the wilderness – can be demythologized if we choose, or done away with as a hangover from a primitive past, but we would be wise not to be too hasty. These references to 'the cosmic powers of this present darkness' and 'spiritual forces of evil in the heavenly places' convey a reality which no amount of educated condescension or bourgeois sophistication can ever match: 'The idea of struggling with the devil points to realities hidden by the cool winds of Enlightenment rationality.'[12] Here is evidence once more, were it needed, that the New Testament is very much a twenty-first-century text.

The powers, though, have been overcome; the devil has been disarmed and his fate has been sealed (Rev. 20.10); it is Christ who is King of kings and Lord of lords. It is he, the blessed redeemer, who will triumph: 'But thanks be to God, who gives us the victory through our Lord Jesus Christ' (1 Cor. 15.57). 'In these things we are more than conquerors through him who loved us' (Rom. 8.37).

The Work of Christ and the Resurrection of Christ

It is through the Holy Spirit that the work of Christ in his lifelong obedience, his costly sacrifice and his dealing with the sins and impurities of a marred creation, become a reality for us and for our world. What the great fourth-century theologian Athanasius called 'the reconciling exchange of Christ'[13] was rooted not only in Christ's obedient life and sacrificial death, but in his resurrection and ascension as well. It was as a human being that Christ was raised again

---

12 Placher, *Jesus the Savior*, p. 147.
13 St Athanasius, *Against the Apollinarians* 1.17, quoted in T. F. Torrance, *The Trinitarian Faith*, p. 165.

on the third day, and his now glorified humanity was taken up into God's eternal presence. Our own fellowship with God and incorporation into Christ is predicated upon that fact: 'You know the grace of our Lord Jesus Christ, that though he was rich yet for your sakes he has become poor that you, through his poverty, might become rich' (2 Cor. 8.9). What eastern Christianity calls *theosis*, 'divinization' or 'participation in God', western Christianity calls fellowship with God or union with Christ. It has nothing to do with mystical loss of one's humanity or a state of sinless perfection, rather it is a matter of being reconciled with God through the blood of Christ. As Christ did not lose his deity in becoming human, so we, in partaking of fellowship with him through repentance and faith, in no way lose our humanity. What happens is that the Word of God, bearing actively upon our human life and consciousness, allows us to believe in Christ, regenerates us in the Spirit and restores in us the image which has been marred by sin. This is what Christian spirituality is all about: it is 'union with God in and through Jesus Christ in whom our human nature is not only saved, healed and renewed but lifted up to participate in the very light, life and love of the Holy Trinity'.[14]

What, then, are we to make of Christ's resurrection from the dead? First of all, it is absolutely essential to the story. Although the narrative which we have considered throughout this book includes creation, incarnation and redemption, none would be complete without the resurrection. Christ's life may be inspiring, his humility may be ennobling and his sacrifice may be chastening, but none would be ultimately significant were it not for the reality of the third day: 'If Christ has not been raised, your faith is futile and you are still in your sins ... If for this life only we have hoped in Christ, we are of all people most to be pitied' (1 Cor.

---

14 Thomas F. Torrance, *The Mediation of Christ*, 2nd edn (Edinburgh: T & T Clark, 1992), p. 66.

15.17, 19). The resurrection is not a 'happy ending' nor is it the product of wish-fulfilment, some sort of delusional recompence or unwarranted optimism for the feeble-minded – the strangeness of the resurrection stories and the disciples' perplexed reaction to the appearances of Christ do not permit this as a valid option. What we do find is, that having penetrated beyond the initial enigma of the risen Christ and the mystery of the empty tomb, the resurrection belongs to the essence of Christian faith: 'this Jesus God raised up, and of that all of us are witnesses' (Acts 2.32).

Jewish beliefs about resurrection were only partial and unfocused during Jesus' day. Not all pious and observant Jews believed in a resurrection; like their forefathers they thought that God's blessing was for this life only and if there was immortality, it would be through their children and their childrens' children. A belief in 'sheol' or the shadowy abode of the dead had developed over time, but it was never central to Old Testament faith, and it was only late in the day, by the time of the Book of Daniel, that any concept of being raised from the dead had made its mark to become one strand in Jewish orthodoxy. Even then resurrection had nothing to do with men's and women's current lives, but with the fate of Israel in a far-off future. So when the disciples were forced to conclude that Christ had been raised from the dead – 'Jesus is alive, he is there to be *encountered* again ... [He] obstinately stands over against us and will not be painlessly assimilated into our own memories'[15] – there was no clear conceptional grid into which this event could be fitted. What was obvious, though, was that Jesus' claims to have spoken with divine authority, and the evidence of his having performed divine acts, were now deemed to be true. It was also apparent that God's final act had, in some way, occurred. The future had intruded into

15 Rowan Williams, *Resurrection: Interpreting the Easter Gospel*, 2nd edn (Harrisburg, Pa: Morehouse Publishing, 1994), pp. 79–80.

the present and God's ultimate purpose was seen to have dawned.

How, then, should the resurrection be interpreted? To think of it in a wooden, static and overly literalistic way would be wrong. The gospel evidence itself is nuanced, oblique and textured: how could it be otherwise? 'A resurrection from the dead, a transformation of the meaning of things, an inbreaking of the ultimate triumph of God into the midst of history – we might expect that such an event would be a little hard to describe.'[16] Were the resurrection stories to be read as straight narrative, they would present us with serious conundrums. Whereas Mark has an empty tomb and no appearances, the apostle Paul has appearances but no empty tomb. Luke mentions a forty-day period during which Jesus walked to Emmaus, made himself known through the breaking of bread and the interpretation of scripture and thereafter ascended to his Father's presence from Bethany. Matthew and John say nothing about forty days but place Christ's appearances in Galilee. Matthew includes the great commission to teach and baptize in the name of the Father, the Son and the Holy Spirit, while John relates the story about the great haul of fish and the doubts of Thomas. Although Christ is known he does not reveal himself simply and directly to his disciples; there is uncertainty and ambiguity and awe. In short we do not have a straightforward text but one in which there are elements of enigma and strangeness. 'The stories themselves', says Rowan Williams, 'are about difficulty, unexpected outcomes, silences, errors, about what is not readily accessible or readily understood.'[17] This is not to say that they are unhistorical or phantom-like apparitions: clearly they were not. What occurred did so in time and place and it is not

16 Placher, *Jesus the Savior*, p. 167.
17 Rowan Williams, *On Christian Theology* (Oxford: Blackwell, 2000), p. 187.

sufficient to claim that the resurrection is a symbolic truth that occurred in the minds and imagination of the disciples with no objective corollary in history. It may be that this history is not amenable to scientific proof – how could it be if its 'proof' derives from some seemingly objective reality beyond God's own self-revelation in Christ? – but history it is, nevertheless.

Not only is it history but it is the key to history. Were our world a closed, mechanistic, godless world, there would be no resurrection and little point and purpose to our lives or the life of our planet. Conversely, were spirituality to be divorced from the living God of scripture who is both beyond creation and has become one with us in Jesus of Nazareth, it too would be locked into the ordinary, the predictable and the mundane. It would certainly have no transcendent reality or saving power. It would also be very boring! What changes all this is the resurrection from the dead. Suddenly possibilities become endless; the creation is open to all sorts of exciting innovations and prospects which are truly radical. We find ourselves in *God's* world which is exhilarating, endlessly fascinating and life itself becomes wholly worthwhile: 'So if anyone is in Christ, there is a new creation; everything old has passed away; see, everything has become new' (2 Cor. 5.17).

Questions for Discussion

1 Do you think that the cross is the most appropriate symbol of our faith?

2 How important is it for you that Jesus Christ has suffered with us as a human being?

3 How relevant is the Old Testament for a contemporary understanding of atonement?

4 Discuss the idea of (a) sacrifice and (b) reconciliation.

5 Why can there be no Christianity without resurrection?

6 Make a list of those things that 'prove' the resurrection.

8

'God's other hand'
The Holy Spirit

Spirit and Trinity

It was the early church father Irenaeus who said that God creates with his two hands: the Word and the Spirit. This chapter will concentrate on the work of the Holy Spirit in creation and in redemption.

For us to know God in an immediate sense and not just at second hand, we need a doctrine of Trinity. This is true now; it was also true when the church devised its doctrine of Trinity during the early Christian centuries. If God, the transcendent Lord, had revealed himself initially as Creator and Redeemer and thence of all things, and if this redemption had been actualized in the incarnation and sacrifice of Jesus Christ, his Son, the question remained as to how God would continue to manifest himself and his saving presence now that Jesus had 'ascended into heaven and is seated at the right hand of the Father'? The New Testament story had already provided an answer to this question in its reporting of the pouring out of the Spirit on the day of Pentecost. Following Christ's resurrection and his ascension into glory, Jesus promised the coming of 'another Advocate (*Paraklētos*)' (John 14.16), sent by the Father to bear witness to the truth: When the Advocate (*Paraklētos*) comes, whom I will send to you from the Father, the Spirit of truth who comes from the Father, he will testify on my behalf' (John 15.26). It was this assertion, conjoined with the Old

Testament prophecy from the Book of Joel whereby God, in the last days, would pour out his spirit on all flesh (Joel 2.28–29), which led to the formation of the concept of the Holy Spirit. With the miraculous phenomenon of Pentecost, this joint promise and prophecy was fulfilled. The disciples were together in a room in Jerusalem when there appeared upon them the tongues of fire and they heard a great rush of the wind; they were transformed from a perplexed and still fearful band of people into a massive missionary force. It was Peter who gave voice to their conviction:

> But Peter, standing with the eleven, raised his voice and addressed them, 'Men of Judea and all who live in Jerusalem, let this be known to you, and listen to what I say ... This is what was spoken through the prophet Joel:
> "In the last days it will be, God declares,
> that I will pour out my Spirit upon all flesh,
>   and your sons and your daughters shall prophesy,
> and your young men shall see visions,
>   and your old men shall dream dreams ...
> Then everyone who calls on the name of the Lord
> shall be saved."' (Acts 2.14–17, 21)

Just as God had revealed himself as Lord and Father of Jesus Christ, and Christ had shown himself to be one with the Father though wholly obedient to him, so the Spirit not only facilitated the ongoing mission of God in the world and among God's people, but also shared in the very nature which bound the Father with the Son. It was the Spirit (not as some emanation from God but somehow separate from God, or as an impersonal divine force), who would continue God's perpetual renewal of creation and also convince the world of sin, righteousness and judgement by glorifying Christ and guiding God's people to all truth (John 16.7–15). Following Pentecost God was perceived as existing as Father, Son *and* Holy Spirit.

The New Testament basis for this truth had already been laid long before the church had formulated its mature doctrine of God as Trinity at the Council of Nicaea in AD 325 and more especially at the Council of Constantinople in AD 381. It was between Pentecost and the Council of Constantinople that the full implications of the Spirit's deity and function within the Trinity were realized, though the worship and practice of the early church already provided an outline of how the orthodox doctrine would actually develop. The command given by the risen Christ to baptize in the name of the Father, the Son *and the Holy Spirit* (Matt. 28.19), which itself sprang from Jesus' own baptism in the Jordan followed by his immediate approval by the Father and anointing *by the Spirit* (Matt. 3.13–17; Mark 1.9–11; Luke 3.21–23), illustrated how this threefold understanding of God would become central for the practice and perpetuation of the apostolic faith. Although the language of 'persons' and 'Trinity' is not found in scripture (as we have seen), the New Testament Epistles especially constantly link 'Father', 'Son', and 'Spirit', attributing the functions of God interchangeably to the three (see Acts 2.32–33; 2 Cor 13.14; Eph. 2.18; 1 Pet. 1.2 etc.). The very life of the church was grounded in the fact that the one single creator and redeemer who had first made himself known to Israel, was now at work in the world imparting God's gracious salvation to humankind through the separate but unified divine 'persons' of Father, Son and Holy Spirit. God remained one God – there were not three gods – but neither were the Father, the Son or the Spirit merely aspects or manifestation of God's one-ness. Each possessed an identity and singularity of its own. At Nicaea this unique relationship between Father and Son had been defined in terms of a co-equal sharing in the divine being or 'substance' (*homoousios*), and after the Council of Constantinople, nearly two generations later, this definition was extended to include the

Spirit. Athanasius of Alexandria, the great champion of the Trinity, found himself defending the personhood of the Spirit against the criticisms of the 'Tropici' – a 'trope' is a metaphor or a figure of speech – a group within the church which was so convinced of the unity of God that they could hardly conceive of the Holy Spirit as a full, distinct, personal and differential entity within God at all. For them, like the modalists we mentioned in Chapter 4, the 'personhood' of the Spirit was a pictorial or metaphorical way of expressing the one God's actions within the world. But for Athanasius this was not the case: 'In ... essence and nature he [the Spirit] is of the Holy Triad.'[1] In other words, the Spirit was not an aspect of God but God's self in a distinct, separate and personal mode which could be differentiated from that of the Father and that of the Son. And if the God the Son was a 'person', that is, a distinct, historical (and eternal) reality apart from the Father, derivative of him but ever obedient to him though sharing in his full deity, the same must be true of the Spirit. After all, did not the scriptures refer to the Spirit as personal: the one who guides (John 16.12), who restrains (Acts 16.6), who distributes his gifts at will (1 Cor. 12.11) and can be saddened and grieved (Eph. 4.30)? For Christ, according to John the Evangelist, the Spirit was 'the *Paraklētos*', a personal being, 'Advocate' or 'Counsellor', and not merely the impersonal *pneuma* or 'spirit'. 'To encounter the Spirit', writes the contemporary theologian Tom Smail, 'is like meeting another person distinct from myself, who indeed enters my experience, but has a life of his own outside my experience and beyond my control.'[2] This was the truth, extrapolated from scripture

---

1 St Athanasius, *First Letter to Serapion on the Holy Spirit*, 27, in C. R. B. Shapland (ed.), *The Letters of Saint Athanasius Concerning the Holy Spirit* (London: Epworth Press, 1951), p. 133.
2 Tom Smail, *The Giving Gift: The Holy Spirit in Person*, 2nd edn (London: Darton, Longman & Todd, 1994), p. 34.

and fully in keeping with the practice of devotion and the logic of faith, which the church expresses in its classical creeds: 'We believe in ... the Holy Spirit, the Lord and life-giver, who proceeds from the Father, who with the Father and Son is together worshipped and together glorified.'[3]

The fact that the one God was seen to coinhere in three separate, divine persons within the Trinity was more than the result of a patient and reverential analysis of scripture. It also conformed to the basic theological axiom that it was only God who could reveal God. 'If the Holy Spirit were a creature', said Athanasius, 'we should have no participation of God in him. If indeed we were joined to a creature, we should be strangers to the divine nature inasmuch as we did not partake therein.'[4] As knowledge of the Father was revealed through the Son who shared deity with him, so knowledge of the Son, who both revealed God and brought about humankind's redemption, could only be mediated through the Spirit. As God can only be known immediately and not at second remove as it were, it follows that the Spirit, too, shares deity with both the Father and the Son.

Between East and West

One of the things we touched upon when discussing the doctrine of the Trinity and the person of Christ was the eternal nature of God the Son: that in the fullness of time Jesus of Nazareth not only revealed the Father and showed us what sort of God he was, but by so doing he claimed something about himself as the Father's perpetual and

---

3 J. N. D. Kelly, *Early Christian Creeds*, 3rd edn (London: Longman, 1972), p. 298.
4 St Athanasius, *First Letter to Serapion on the Holy Spirit* 24, in Shapland (ed.), *The Letters of Saint Athanasius Concerning the Holy Spirit*, p. 126.

ever-existing Son. 'The Father and I are one' (John 10.30).
If this was the case, that Christ shared deity with the Father
and that the Father had existed in eternity long before the
creation of the world, it followed, surely, that in some mysterious way, the Son too had always been.

The gospel evidence pointed in the same direction: 'Very
truly, I tell you, before Abraham was I am' (John 8.58). The
'I am' here is the divine 'I am', the Old Testament ascription
of God which Jesus Christ took for himself according to
the Gospel of John. In the great high priestly prayer uttered
in Jerusalem just before his passion, Christ again makes the
same claim: 'So now, Father, glorify me in your presence
with the glory that I had in your presence before the world
existed' (John 17.5). The way in which the church formulated its belief about the eternal existence of God the Son
was through the idea of the Logos, the divine Word. 'In the
beginning was the Word, and the Word was with God, and
the Word was God' (John 1.1). God had never been simply
'alone'; in the depths of eternity, before time began, God
existed in plurality, in co-fraternity, in community. God *is*
community and he always has been so, the blessed fellowship of Father, Son and Holy Spirit. At a specific juncture
in history, in a particular time and in a definite place, God
the Word conjoined himself to humanity in the person of
Jesus of Nazareth, the human son of Mary. The Anglo-
Welsh theologian A. M. Allchin expresses the mystery of
incarnation, and all its implications for our lives, in a very
striking way:

God enters into the material world. He is present at the
roots of humanity's affective, natural, bodily life. The
fullness of the deity is revealed not only in the mind and
the speech of Jesus, but in his body, that which he took
from us, that in which he is most with us. The most basic
of human experiences, of needs and satisfactions, ful-

filments and anxieties are the soil in which the divine is revealed and grows. Every human act, rooted in the material, animal order, part of the material world and sharing much with the animal creation, can yet become fully human, in becoming free and consciously realized, can indeed be known as a gift, discovered as a response of thanks to God, can be divine. Grace shines through, illuminates and transfigures the human order in its totality, shows that it has a wholly unsuspected goal and destiny; for God has entered into the very processes of birth.[5]

Yet the point is not that Jesus *became* the Son of God but in the fullness of time, at this particular place in history, the eternal Son of God became one with humankind *in* the person of Jesus of Nazareth. This manifestation in time and place, within the flow of humanity's long and sorry story, made plain what had already been true about God in eternity, that the Father had always been the Father of the Son and the Son had always been 'begotten of the Father before all ages'. What was antecedently true of God as Father and as Son now became historically true in the birth of Jesus Christ to Mary, his mother, in the township of Bethlehem on the west bank of the River Jordan. 'If we are to speak truly of the God we confess,' remarked Colin Gunton, 'we must make Jesus in someway intrinsic to his being, and that requires insisting that he is eternally begotten.'[6]

The word used here is 'begotten', a word which alludes to the specific relationship between Father and Son within the unity of the one God. But what has this to do with the Spirit? Just as the word 'begotten' was used of the Son in

5 A. M. Allchin, *The Joy of all Creation: An Anglican Meditation on the Place of Mary*, 2nd edn (London: New City, 1993), p. 18.
6 Colin E. Gunton, *Father, Son and Holy Spirit: Towards a Full Trinitarian Theology* (London: T & T Clark, 2003), p. 70.

his eternal relationship with the Father, the word 'procession' came to be used of the Spirit in *his* eternal relation to the Father and the Son. 'When the Advocate (*Parakletos*) comes, whom I will send to you from the Father, the Spirit of truth who comes (*ekporeuetai* = 'proceeds') from the Father, he will testify on my behalf' (John 15.26). And that takes us to the difference in understanding of the Spirit which exists between the Eastern Church and that of the West. For the Eastern Church, the Greek-speaking chuches of the ancient Christian centres of Jerusalem, Constantinople, Alexandria and Antioch which spread into the Slavic lands and Russia, the Spirit, although eternal and divine, derives his being from the Father alone. The Father is the source or fount of the deity; he is the one who (as scripture affirms) has precedence over all, the one from whom Christ came and to whom Christ returned, the one to whom Jesus prayed and gave his full obedience, and as this was true of the earthly Christ, it is surely true of the eternal Son or Word. The Spirit, therefore, like the Son, though fully personal and wholly divine, derives *his* essence also from the Father alone. For the Western Church, on the other hand, the Latin-speaking church of Rome, North Africa and all parts of Europe to the east of Greece, what is essential about God is the full and complete sharing of deity between Father and Son. There is but one God in whom both Father and Son share the same divine nature and essence. Because of this complete parity and eternal unity, what is true of the Father must be true of the Son. Therefore the Spirit, while co-eternal and co-divine with both Father and Son, derives his existence from them both. The Father is inconceivable without the Son and the Son does nothing independently of the Father, therefore for the Western Church of St Augustine, the North African theologian and the greatest of the Latin fathers, the Spirit 'proceeds' from both the Father *and* the Son. In the Middle Ages, the phrase *filioque*, 'from the Son', was inserted (unilaterally, by the Bishop of Rome) into the Latin version of the Nicene Creed: 'We believe in ... the Holy Spirit, the Lord and giver of life, who proceeds from the Father *and the Son (filioque)*, who with the Father and the Son together is worshipped and glorified.'[7] This led to the grievous schism between Rome and the East, and as the sixteenth-century Reformation was a solely European matter which occured within the bounds of the Catholic church of the West, the Protestant churches – the Anglicans, the Lutherans and the Reformed (including the orthodox Nonconformists in England and Wales) – have, in the main, followed the western lead.

What, then, is the significance of this development for our understanding of the Spirit and our knowledge of God? It would seem that the East has scripture on its side when it emphasizes the precedence of the Father. The most bald statement of the priority of the Father and corresponding subordination of the Son is to be found in Jesus' response to the rich young ruler in the Gospel of Mark: 'Why do you call me good? No one is good but God alone' (Mark 10.18). Even the Johannine material (which is least susceptible to a subordinist interpretation) regularly cites the primacy of the Father: 'Very truly, I tell you, the Son can do nothing on his own, but only what he sees the Father doing; for whatever the Father does, the Son does likewise' (John 5.19); and again, 'If you loved me, you would rejoice that I am going to the Father, because the Father is greater than I' (John 14.28). This chimes in well with the words of the apostle Paul who also highlights the priority of God the Father. It is, by implication, God *the Father* who has 'poured out his love into our hearts by the Holy Spirit whom he has given us' (Rom. 5.3). The climax of the redemption wrought by the risen Christ is that 'every tongue should confess that

---

7 Kelly, *Early Christian Creeds*, p. 358.

Jesus Christ is Lord, to the glory of God *the Father*' (Phil. 2.11). At the end times, it is God the Father, for Paul, who will receive all glory:

> Then comes the end, when [Christ] hands over the king-dom *to God the Father* ... When all things are subjected to him, then the Son himself will also be subjected to the one who put all things in subjection under him, so that God may be all in all. (1 Cor. 15.24, 28)

Just as the Father has priority over the Son, scripture also suggests that the Spirit is in a subordinate position as well: 'When the Advocate (*Paraklētos*) comes, whom I will send to you *from the Father*, the Spirit of truth who comes *from the Father*, he will testify on my behalf' (John 15.26).

Along with this ostensibly biblical emphasis on the Father's absolute priority within the Godhead, the East-ern Church has often criticized the western tradition for depersonalizing the Spirit. By putting such a great stress on the co-equality of the Father and the Son, the tendency has been to allow the Spirit to be eclipsed or to be treated as less than fully personal. For St Augustine the Spirit was the bond which joined together the Father and the Son within the community of the Holy Trinity or 'the mutual love whereby the Father and the Son love one another'.[8] This being the case there is little wonder that the theolo-gians of the East saw western trinitarianism as downgrad-ing the Spirit's personhood. For the emigré Russian thinker Vladimir Lossky, 'By the dogma of the *Filioque*, the God of the philosophers and savants is introduced into the heart of the Living God.'[9] The Spirit, he claims, has become an

---

8 St Augustine, *The Trinity* 15.27, in Henry Bettenson (ed.), *The Later Christian Fathers* (Oxford: Oxford University Press, 1970), p. 229.
9 Vladimir Lossky, *In the Image and Likeness of God* (New York: St Vladimir's Seminary Press, 1985), p. 88.

abstraction or a non-personal effect between Father and Son and consequently merely an 'influence' within the world. A less polemic though no less pointed critique is made by the Orthodox Bishop Kallistos Ware:

> The Latins, while affirming the divinity of the Spirit, have failed to appreciate sufficiently his distinct personality. As a result of the *filioque* they have tended to treat the Spirit as a function and instrument of the Son, and not as a sovereign and co-equal person in his own right. This has meant that inadequate attention is paid in western theology to the work of the Spirit, in the world, in the life of the church and in the daily experience of each Christian.[10]

It has often been said that the authoritarian and unbending streak in Western Christianity, whether represented by the infallibility of the Pope or a rigid church discipline within Catholicism, a mechanical doctrine of the ministry and sacraments within Anglicanism, or rationalistic concepts such as the inerrancy of scripture in conservative Protestantism, is a direct consequence of this depersonalizing of the Spirit. A reaction was bound to set in, and it hardly seems surprising that such spontaneous spiritual interruptions as pietism, revivalism, as well as pentecostalism and charismatic renewal, are characteristics of the *Western* Church rather than the Church of the East. Nineteenth-century theological liberalism with its protest in favour of the sovereign freedom of the human spirit can also be viewed in this light. In the words of Tom Smail:

> The subordination of the Holy Spirit to the Son in western Christendom is by no means confined to the exotic

---

10 Kallistos Ware in H. Cunliffe-Jones (ed.), *A History of Christian Doctrine* (Edinburgh: T & T Clark, 1978), p. 211.

technicalities of trinitarian theology, but goes on mani-
festing itself in all sorts of ways in the life and worship
of the churches.[11]

But this is not the only way to read the evidence. Although the New Testament seems to point to the Father's
precedence within the being of God, the position of the Son
is, nevertheless, wholly central to that same being. There is
no Father apart from the Son and scripture also refers to
the fact that it is *the Son* who sends the Spirit: 'When the
Advocate (*Paraklētos*) comes, whom *I* will send from the
Father' (John 15.26); 'It is to your advantage that I go away,
for if I do not go away, the Advocate will not come to you;
but if I go, *I* will send him to you' (John 16.7). If the Father
is the source of God's being, the Spirit is never sent from
that source alone: he is sent *from* the Father *by* the Son.
There is no independent 'procession' or sending: Father
and Son work in harmony or they do not work at all: 'He
[the Spirit] will glorify me [the Son], because he will take
what is mine and declare it to you. All that the Father has
is mine' (John 16.14–15). It is very striking that at the end
of the Gospel of John, it is not the Father directly but the
risen Christ who imparts the Spirit to the disciples: ' "As
the Father has sent me, so I send you". When he had said
this, he breathed on them and said to them, "Receive the
Holy Spirit"' (John 20.22). The whole thrust of the apostolic witness shows that the Spirit, even if he does spring
ultimately from the Father, never bypasses the Son but in
fact works with, through and for the Son. From Pentecost
onwards, when Peter's sermon centred not on the Father or
on the Spirit but on 'Jesus of Nazareth, a man attested to
you by God with deeds of power, wonders, and signs that
God did through him among you' (Acts 2.22), Christ, his

---

11 Smail, *The Giving Gift*, p. 135.

person and work, remains the focus for the Spirit's work and what is true of the Son in history is true of him in eternity as well.

Where does this leave us? It strikes me as quite reasonable that the Western Church would want to ensure the Son's centrality in its concept of God and consequently the Holy Spirit's ministry as having proceeded from both the Father *and* the Son. If our doctrine of God is not Christ-centred, it is not adequately Christian. If the western idea can be accused of depersonalizing the Spirit and thinking of him as an influence or an effect, the eastern idea is also open to abuse. Even such an unstinting apologist for Orthodoxy as Vladimir Lossky admitted as much: 'It may be asked whether, in seeking to avoid the semi-Sabellianism of the Latins, their Greek adversaries did not fall into subordinationism because of their emphasis on the monarchy of the Father.'[12] (This sounds very technical! The 'monarchy of the Father' refers to the Father's precedence within the being of God; 'subordinationism' means an over-gradation between the three persons of the Trinity which turns them, effectively, into three gods; and 'semi-Sabellianism' is the idea that the three persons of the Trinity are merely three non-personal aspects of the one God.) Although Lossky refutes the charge, nevertheless it does have some force: 'If the eastern Orthodox position has a great strength, it also has a great weakness: it does not make sufficiently clear how the coming of the Spirit is cradled in and dependent upon the work of the Son.'[13] In this invitation to doctrine, we need to keep Christ central not only in redemption and creation but in our knowledge and understanding of the very being of God; and if God consists of the eternal fellowship of Father, Son and Holy Spirit, we cannot afford to divorce the work of the Spirit from the person of the Son.

12 Lossky, *In the Image and Likeness of God*, p. 81.
13 Smail, *The Giving Gift*, p. 124.

It may be that the Spirit has his source in the Father but the Spirit finds a focus in both the eternal Son and the historical Christ. And this, as we shall see, has implications for our understanding of our world as well as of our God. Not only does the Holy Spirit reveal who God is in Christ, but he also draws us to God's good creation too.

Spirit and Creation

As the Spirit shares in God's essence and nature, and as God exists apart from the world, God's presence *within* his world can be understood in terms of the presence of God's Spirit. As the world's creator and Lord, God remains transcendent. He never so immerses himself in the world as to become an undifferentiated part of it; this would be the belief of the pantheists who would seek to deify creation and blur the distinction between humankind (and animalkind) and God. For a sound Christian theology this is not an option. Yet it is surely true to claim that God manifests his presence within the world and very often his glory as well. You only have to turn to the Old Testament nature Psalms to see how regularly this fact is expressed:

> The heavens are telling the glory of God;
>   and the firmament proclaims his handiwork.
> Day to day pours forth speech,
>   and night to night declares knowledge. (Ps. 19.1–2)

God remains transcendent, but the glory of this transcendent God is revealed in the living things that he has made. Creation is not some static, once-and-for-all occurrence divorced from the perpetual reality of the living God. God upholds his creation and renews it constantly through his presence as Spirit. This truth was expressed, with customary clarity, by the great Genevan Reformer John Calvin:

For it is the Spirit who, everywhere diffused, sustains all things, causes them to grow, and quickens them in heaven and in earth. Because he is circumscribed by no limits, he is excepted from the category of creatures; but is transfusing into all things his energy, and breathing into them essence, life, and movement. He is, indeed, plainly divine.[14]

Although God remains God, and as such is categorically different from God's creation, it is he who is the source of that creation and all that flourishes within it. His presence is the immanent presence, through the Spirit, of the transcendent God.

In the Old Testament the Spirit was depicted as a dynamic force, given by God, which breathed life into creation and animated all things. This is well stated in some of the nature Psalms:

O LORD, how manifold are your works!
  In wisdom you have made them all;
  the earth is full of your creatures ...
These all look to you
  to give them their food in due season ...
When you take away their breath, they die
  and return to their dust.
When you send forth your spirit, they are created;
  and you renew the face of the ground.
                    (Ps. 104.24, 27, 29b–30)

It was this spirit which existed from the beginning as the Spirit of creation who, when the earth was in darkness and without form, moved over the face of the waters: 'In the

14 John Calvin, *Institutes of the Christian Religion* 1.13.14 (Philadelphia: Westminster Press, 1960), p. 138.

beginning when God created the heavens and the earth, the earth was a formless void and darkness covered the face of the deep, while the spirit of God swept over the face of the waters' (Gen. 1.1–2). Creation, though in an absolute way the work of God, needed to be brought to perfection; the initial chaos still awaited to be fashioned into a cosmos. The divine Word having created still needed to instil order and harmony into that which, although created, was yet characterized as a chaotic void. A sovereign process had begun which required time to be brought to fullness and completion; in seven days God would turn this formless (though created) void into a lush, flourishing construct teeming with life. It is, surely, no coincidence that the author links this continuing act of creation with the presence of the *ruach elohim*, 'the spirit [or breath] of God'. Neither is it a coincidence that the second creation account in Genesis 2 states that Adam was made from the dust of the earth and was animated by the same spirit of life: 'Then the LORD God formed man from the dust of the ground, and breathed into his nostrils the breath of life; and the man became a living being' (Gen. 2.7).

We heed hardly labour the point that this 'spirit' is not the Holy Spirit, the third person of the Trinity, co-substantial with Father and Son. It was not until the New Testament that the church was provided with the wherewithal to develop its doctrine of the Trinity. We should have no qualms, however, about seeing these references, and others like them, as preparing the way for a developed and legitimate doctrine of Trinity in which the 'spirit' is not so much an impersonal spirit of deity but the personal and specific reality within God through which God expresses his creative design. It is of the essence of that creative intent to infuse all things with life: 'The spirit of God has made me', claimed that wise, if unfortunate, character, Job, 'and the breath of the Almighty gives me life' (Job 33.4).

Thus says God, the LORD,
> who created the heavens and stretched them out,
> who spread out the earth and what comes from it,
who gives breath to the people upon it
> and spirit to those who walk in it. (Isa. 42.5)

By the word of the LORD the heavens were made,
> and all their host by the breath of his mouth. (Ps. 33.6)

The whole of creation, including humankind, is animated by the spirit of life and it derives its vitality directly from the sovereign Lord, God the Spirit.

In turning to the New Testament the same conviction is sustained but, as always, finds a new focus and centre. In the Old Testament the spirit had been, mostly, that which had animated creation and bestowed upon mortal beings life. The Spirit had interpenetrated and quickened creation and was present therein as the immanent presence of Yahweh, the still transcendent Lord. It was upon him that all people derived their existence and remained dependent; in him we all 'live and move and have our being' (Acts 17.28). It was not often that the Spirit was seen as the source of spiritual or resurrection life. It is true that the judges, kings and prophets were anointed by God for specific tasks and the 'spirit of the LORD came upon' them (e.g. Judg. 11.9) though that spirit, more often than not, was withdrawn when their responsibilities were complete. There are, however, hints of the Spirit imparting something more akin to immortality than the breath of earthly life. The prophet Ezekiel's magnificent vision of the renewal of Israel refers to the Spirit as the source of mortal, created life *and* the life of the world to come:

Then he said to me, 'Prophesy to the breath, prophesy, mortal, and say to the breath: Thus says the Lord GOD:

Come from the four winds, O breath, and breathe upon
these slain that they may live ...'

Then he said to me, 'Mortal, these bones are the whole
house of Israel. They say, "Our bones are dried up, and
our hope is lost; we are cut off completely." Therefore
prophesy, and say to them, Thus says the Lord GOD: I
am going to open your graves, and bring you up from
your graves, O my people; and I will bring you back to
the land of Israel.' (Ezek. 37.9, 11–12)

Along with the prophecy of Joel which we mentioned at
the beginning of the chapter, this was the link between the
Old Testament concept of the Spirit as animating the whole
of creation and the way that the Spirit, in the New Testament, becomes an eschatological reality pointing to the life
of the world to come. These are not mutually exclusive,
neither does one supersede the other; the Spirit remains the
Spirit of creation, God at work in everyday things imparting goodness, order, beauty and power. But now the Spirit
becomes the Spirit of redemption as well, that which has to
do with explicitly spiritual matters.

The focus for all this, as we should expect, is Jesus
Christ. Just as the world was created *ex nihilo*, 'out of nothing', so does God create anew through the Holy Spirit, and
he begins with Christ. The Christian tradition has been
adamant about the means of Christ's conception: it was
through the Holy Spirit. 'Now the birth of Jesus the Messiah took place this way. When his mother Mary had been
engaged to Joseph, but before they lived together, she was
found to be with child from the Holy Spirit' (Matt. 1.18).
The Gospel of Luke expresses the same truth by stating,
of Mary, that 'The Holy Spirit will come upon you, and
the power of the Most High will overshadow you' (Luke
1.35). This was a birth 'not of blood or of the will of the
flesh or of the will of man, but of God' (John 1.13). This

may be a miracle and a mystery but it is no more a mystery than that of creation or of resurrection. It belongs to the same category of reality and is of a piece with both facts. It should be taken seriously and not be mythologized away. 'The doctrine of the virginal conception reminds us that this new life does not arise out of the earth, which is, along with us, fallen. It can arise only by the recreating act of the God who called light out of darkness.'[15] Here, as elsewhere, the Spirit has to do with creation; it does not bypass matter or the flesh but is involved intimately with both. In the incarnation of the Son, the Father made particular his creative will through the action of the Spirit and he did it for our redemption. As Colin Gunton says: 'The incarnation represents among other things a particular use of the created order by the Father through the Spirit, in forming a body of flesh for his eternal Son.'[16] In so doing 'God the Father through his Spirit shapes this representative sample of the natural world for the sake of the remainder of it.'[17] This action is not self-contained. It occurs in conjunction with the created world, in this case humankind, and for the sake of that same created world. Here, in Christ, the Spirit has to do with creation.

What is true of the incarnation of the Son of God is equally true of his whole ministry, his death and resurrection. The Spirit was active throughout his life, setting him apart to fulfil his mission through his baptism by John in the Jordan and remained present in all his actions. It was by the Spirit that he was led into the wilderness to be tempted by Satan (Matt. 4.1); it was through the Spirit that he cast out demons, thus restoring God's good, though marred, creation to its original state (Matt. 12.28); it was through

15 Colin E. Gunton, *Theology through Preaching* (Edinburgh: T & T Clark, 2001), p. 71.
16 Gunton, *Father, Son and Holy Spirit*, p. 116.
17 Gunton, *Father, Son and Holy Spirit*, p. 117.

the Spirit that he preached his message about the coming of God's eschatological kingdom: 'Then Jesus, filled with the power of the Spirit, returned to Galilee, and a report about him spread through all the surrounding country. He began to teach in their synagogues and was praised by everyone' (Luke 4.14; cf. v.18).

The same was true of his death and his being raised from the dead. It was 'through the eternal Spirit' that he 'offered himself without blemish to God' in order to effect our redemption (Heb. 9.14) while the resurrection occurred in the realm of created, historical, material reality but through the instrumentality of the Spirit (Rom. 1.4). Although he was 'put to death in the flesh, [he was] made alive in the Spirit' (1 Pet. 2.18). This resurrection, in accordance with the same principle of creation through the Spirit, is a *physical* resurrection, whereby the Lord, the giver of life, transforms the body of Christ so that it partakes of the new age, the life of the world to come; he is the firstborn of the new creation. And if that was true of Christ, it will be true of those who believe in him also: 'If the Spirit of him who raised Jesus from the dead dwells in you, he who raised Christ from the dead will give life to your mortal bodies also through his Spirit that dwells in you' (Rom. 8.11).

The implications of all this are obvious: God involves himself in the fleshly, material, mudane realities of creation and he does so in the Spirit, while Christ, the eternal Son of God, is equally involved in all aspects of this created world. The Spirit, therefore, should not be seen principally in relation to Christ's divinity; it has more to do with his humanity, that which joins him to the rest of the created world. It was the Spirit who enabled him, hemmed in as he was by a fallen humanity, to live a sinless life according to the will of God. 'We make Christ free of all stain', remarked Calvin, 'not just because he was begotten of his mother without copulation with man, but because he was sanctified by the

Spirit that the generation might be pure and undefiled as would have been true before Adam's fall.'[18] The Holy Spirit remains the Spirit of creation, God's dynamic and lifegiving power towards the world, even as he empowers the Son of God in all his humanity. As it was fallen flesh that Christ assumed in order to redeem humankind from sin, death and corruption, it was the Spirit that maintained him in sinlessness throughout his work of redemption. The Spirit in Christ, therefore, is not so much an immanent endowment rooted in his divinity, but the sovereign action of God upon him and with him which enables the incarnate Son to fulfil his tasks: 'God the Spirit opens, frees, the humanity of the Son so that it may be the vehicle of the Father's will in the world.'[19]

There is one more thing that we need to mention in the context of the Spirit's involvement in creation; it has to do with the renewal not just of individuals and humankind in Christ but of the remainder of a marred though still good creation as well. Paul mentions it in his letter to the Romans:

> For the creation was subjected to futility, not by its own will but by the will of the one who subjected it, in hope that the creation itself will be set free from its bondage to decay and and will obtain the freedom of the glory of the children of God. (Rom. 8.20–21)

Redemption is not individualistic but corporate; it has less to do with isolated individuals than with the whole theatre of God's glory. Christ, once more, is the key, which takes us to our final section in this chapter, the Holy Spirit and redemption.

---

18 Calvin, *Institutes of the Christian Religion* 2.13.4, p. 481.
19 Colin E. Gunton, 'The Spirit in the Trinity', in Alasdair I. C. Heron (ed.), *The Forgotten Trinity* (London: British Council of Churches, 1991), p. 127.

The Spirit and Redemption

Whereas the early church of the East and the West spent much time in discussing the deity of the Holy Spirit and his status within the being of God, it was after the Protestant Reformation that Christian thinkers gave special attention to the way in which the Spirit transformed human life. 'Mainstream Protestant theology preserved and maintained the established western *doctrine*', wrote Alasdair Heron, 'but at the same time concentrated with a new intensity on what the Spirit *enables* and *performs*.'[20] It was as though interest shifted from who God was to what God does; from the Spirit as being divine to the Spirit as an active reality imparting gifts to individuals, making them holy and engendering fruits in their lives. It is notable that the classic study of the doctrine of the Holy Spirit among the seventeenth-century Puritans hardly ever mentions the being of God as Trinity and never once the *filioque* clause, but has much to say about the felt nearness of God, 'heart religion' and peoples' *experience* of the divine. 'The interest is not primarily dogmatic, at least not in any theoretic sense,' says its author, 'it is experiential. There is a theology, but, in a way which has hardly been known since St Augustine, it is a *theologia pectoris* ("a theology of the heart")'.[21]

Because of this the doctrine of the Holy Spirit among most modern western Christians has been connected with religious experience and subjective feelings, the culture of the 'saved soul', and only obliquely with the objective reality of God or with the call to exercise sovereignty over social and political matters within God's world. Both extremes seem excessive. A balanced doctrine of the Spirit

---

20 Alasdair I. C. Heron, *The Holy Spirit* (Philadelphia: Westminster Press, 1983), p. 99.
21 Geoffrey F. Nuttall, *The Holy Spirit in Puritan Faith and Experience*, 2nd edn (Chicago: University of Chicago Press, 1992), p. 7.

will keep together God *and* his blessings; individual salvation *and* corporate redemption; the present renewal of
creation through social, cultural and political involvement
and an openness to God's future through experiences of
prayer, praise, pentecostal fervour and charismatic gifts.
Holiness is an embodied holiness, which never takes us out
of the world but which renews us in its very midst.

What, then, of the Holy Spirit and redemption? The Spirit
is the Holy Spirit of regeneration, renewal and promise. In
becoming incarnate, the Son took upon himself the corruption of humankind, and through his obedience, sacrifice
and resurrection, became the firstborn and herald of the
new creation, the new heaven and the new earth in which
righteousness will dwell. Not only did Jesus Christ receive
the Holy Spirit but also he imparted it to others baptiz-
ing them 'with the Holy Spirit and with fire' (Matt. 3.11).
The pouring out of the Spirit at Pentecost inaugurated the
arrival of God's kingdom, however partial, within human
history. Thereafter the Christian life of communion with
Christ is essentially life in the Spirit (Rom. 8.1–8; 1 Cor.
12–13; Gal. 5.16–26 etc.). It is the Spirit who induces repentance, creates faith and imparts to individuals the spirit
of adoption whereby they become children of God and
members of God's family:

> For you did not receive a spirit of slavery to fall back into
> fear, but you have received a spirit of adoption. When
> we cry 'Abba! Father!' it is that very Spirit bearing wit-
> ness with our spirit that we are children of God. (Rom.
> 8.15–16)

> And because you are children, God has sent the Spirit of
> his Son into our hearts, crying 'Abba! Father!' So you are
> no longer a slave but a child, and if a child then also an
> heir, through God. (Gal. 4.6–7)

It was not for nothing that the apostle Paul claimed that 'God's love has been poured out into our hearts through the Holy Spirit' (Rom. 5.5). It is through the Spirit that we are born anew, incorporated through baptism into the body of Christ: 'For in the one Spirit we were all baptized into one body – Jews or Greeks, slaves or free – and we were all made to drink of one Spirit' (1 Cor. 12.13); it is through the Spirit that we receive the seal of promise: 'In him you also, when you had heard the word of truth, the gospel of your salvation, and had beleived in him, were marked with the seal of the promised Holy Spirit' (Eph. 1.13), while the Spirit allows us to bring forth those virtues and qualities that Paul calls spiritual 'fruits': love, joy, peace, patience, kindness, goodness, faithfulness, gentleness and self-control (Gal. 5.22–23). In the Spirit we are allowed to partake of the assurance of God's ultimate victory over sin, death and evil whereby we will be resurrected and transformed in order to inherit the fullness of God's kingdom which Christ, on the last day, will deliver to the Father and God will be all in all (1 Cor. 15.20–28).

The key, as we have said, is Christ, and Christ, as we have seen, is not only the eternal Word of God but also part of God's creation. The Spirit is the one who animates creation and who justifies and sanctifies creation as well. In his resurrection through the power of the Spirit, Christ has opened the way forward for humankind and oriented the whole of creation towards the future. God's good creation is not a closed box in which nothing new or unexpected can happen, but an open, joyful, expectant and hope-laden entity which has been made free: 'Now the Lord is the Spirit, and where the Spirit of the Lord is, there is freedom' (2 Cor. 3.17). It also yearns for that freedom which it already knows in part, to become an accomplished fact:

We know that the whole creation has been groaning in labour pains until now; and not only the creation but we ourselves, who have the first fruits of the Spirit, groan inwardly while we wait for adoption, the redemption of our bodies. (Rom. 8.22–23)

So the Spirit instills a hope which brings together Christ, the wider creation and ourselves, while Christ remains the one in whose image all are recast. In other words, the Spirit's mission is to sanctify and redeem creation according to God's purpose and for God's use:

> He is the saint-making Spirit. Saints are on the one hand true to themselves, their times and their culture. They are inexplicable except in terms of the blood they inherit and the soil from which they spring.
> Out of that material, respecting all that is of God in it, the creator Spirit brings forth a new likeness of Jesus. There are no stereotypes of sanctity. All the saints are gloriously various, but out of all the differing colours and textures of their created natures and personalities the Spirit sets himself to paint a new ikon of the Lord. Being thus in the process of being recreated by the Spirit, saints begin to be themselves recreative in the communities and societies to which they belong.[22]

The gift of the Spirit for our sanctification and for the redemption of the whole of creation is not given alone; it creates fellowship and a new way of being community. And that takes us forward to a discussion of the church.

---

22 Smail, *The Giving Gift*, p. 180.

Questions for Discussion

1 Do you think of the Holy Spirit as an 'influence' or as a 'person'?

2 How best can we relate the Holy Spirit to God the Father and God the Son?

3 Think of the examples of the work of the Holy Spirit in the life of Jesus (his conception, his baptism, his resurrection), and discuss their significance for your understanding of his life and work.

4 Give some examples of the activity of the Holy Spirit in God's creation.

5 Make a list of the fruits of the Spirit in Galatians 6, and discuss their importance in your life.

6 In which way does the Spirit create a new ideal of community?

9

The Body of Christ
The Community of the Church

The Foundation of the Church

The revelation which we have considered, prefigured in the Old Testament, culminating in the New Testament with Christ, his death, resurrection and ascension into heaven, affirmed at Pentecost by the witness of the apostles, and appropriated through the Holy Spirit by faith, does not occur in a void. Indeed, through the preaching of God's redemptive word not merely individuals but a new people is called into being, 'a chosen race, a royal priesthood, a holy nation, God's own people' (1 Pet. 2.9). This community is called the church, a gathering together of those who are called by God, grafted by baptism into the body of Christ, who witness to God's reality in the Holy Spirit and reflect Christ's presence in the world. Such is 'the household of God, which is the church of the living God, the pillar and bulwark of the truth' (1 Tim. 3.15).

It is the easiest thing in the world to knock and mock the church and point to the discrepancies between the high-blown claims which scripture makes for it and the prosaic and sometimes corrupt worldliness of its historical manifestation. 'The reference to the church in connection with the idea of perfection', writes Colin Gunton, 'may well induce a hollow laugh in the modern world.'[1] But it is not the

---

1 Colin E. Gunton, *The Christian Faith: An Introduction to Christian Doctrine* (Oxford: Blackwell, 2002), p. 119.

world but the church itself that has been most conscious of its own imperfections and its need for renewal and repentance, a renewal which, time and again, has been granted: 'The strange thing about the church is not that it grows old, but that it seems to have discovered the secret of being born again.'[2] A history of twenty centuries of growth and vitality, which, some parts of present-day Europe excepted, show no signs of abating, is quite remarkable in the history of civilization. It could well be claimed that it was not the presence of Christianity but its absence which caused many of the horrors of the last century:

> It cannot be said too often that the wholesale murder of millions of people by self-consciously atheist regimes and the personal, social and ecological damage inflicted on the world by our secular culture alike suggest that, however damaging this religion can be, its rejection has produced frightful evil.[3]

Despite its manifold and manifest weaknesses, it is the church that has proved itself to be a nursery for saints and the mother of the faithful. It was not a devout Christian but a sceptic from an earlier generation who claimed that 'the belief in this crucified carpenter has taken more men out of themselves than any other thing in all recorded history'.[4] To do that it needed a church. It is the church that has provided a context for and manifestation of sincere worship, vital belief, humanitarian concern and not infrequently selfless practice. These things have invariably occurred from the midst of a community.

---

2 Daniel T. Jenkins, *The Strangeness of the Church* (London: Victor Gollancz, 1956), p. 14.
3 Gunton, *The Christian Faith*, p. 120.
4 The historian G. G. Coulton, quoted in T. E. B. Howarth, *Cambridge Between Two Wars* (London: Collins, 1978), p. 50.

The communal response to God's gracious call in the gospel is explicit throughout the Bible. In Genesis 12 God called Abraham. Abraham was not a solitary individual but the father and founder of the nation. God's promises are not made to him alone but to his descendants: 'Go from your country and your kindred and your father's house to the land that I will show you. I will make of you a great nation' (Gen. 12.1–2a). It was this nation of Israel that became the focus for God's redemptive plan in the Old Testament and not isolated individuals. Faith was the faith of the *people* and obedient response occurred in the context of the *community* of the redeemed.

This theme of obedient response and communal faith was developed in a decisive manner with the redemptive reality of the exodus. It was the exodus from Egypt and its related events which formed Israel into a conscious community with a definite purpose which set it apart from the other nations and gave it a pattern of life which equipped it to fulfil that purpose. The nomadic descendants of Abraham, a small and insignificant grouping among the tribes of Egypt, were galvanized into a renewed identity by God's call, this time through Moses. Through him God delivered his people from bondage. At Sinai he called them to solemn assembly. In his commandments the word was proclaimed. As a community they covenanted together to do his will and obey his words: 'Everything that the LORD has spoken we will do' (Exod. 19.8). Having ratified the covenant with a sacrifice, the people affirmed the communal nature of their faith.

God's relation with his people is understood in terms of covenant, not a contract, a bargain between equals, but a statement of sheer, undeserved grace, including God's everlasting promise to protect and bless these his people. Ever and again this covenant is broken; ever and again the people, denounced by the prophets, are called back to repentance and hope. Despite the apostasy of the majority, the people of God survive and their communal nature is preserved by the remnant, those within the larger body who have observed the conditions of the covenant and remained faithful to its precepts. The remnant would soon become the focus for God's purpose not only for Israel but for the whole of humankind. So despite faithfulness having led to exile, in Babylon this time rather than Egypt, exile hails a new exodus and a new deliverance with the prophetic voices of Jeremiah, Ezekiel and the later Isaiah sounding forth hope for a brighter future, a new intervention of God, the speaking of a final saving word, the accomplishment of an ultimate redemptive action, the establishment of a greater covenant. This new intervention of God's would incorporate the witness of the remnant. Moreover it would no longer be an external covenant, written on tablets of stone, but an internal covenant written on the hearts of the people:

> The days are surely coming, says the LORD, when I will make a new covenant with the house of Israel and the house of Judah. It will not be like the covenant that I made with their ancestors when I took them by the hand to bring them out of the land of Egypt – a covenant that they broke, though I was their husband, says the LORD. But this is the covenant that I will make with the house of Israel after those days, says the LORD: I will put my law within them, and I will write it on their hearts; and I will be their God, and they shall be my people. (Jer. 31.31–33)

In the fullness of time God indeed acted once and for all in the person of Jesus Christ, a son of Israel, the elect nation and Servant of the Lord (Isa. 41.8–10; 42.1–4). This Jesus was recognized by some as the Messiah, sent by God to be the promised deliverer of the people, who embodied the faithful remnant in himself at its starkest point, in his solitary sacrifice on Calvary. It was there, having been judged by God in the place of his sinful people, that he fulfilled the role of mediator of the new covenant between God and them. Jesus saw himself as Israel, the sole representative of the righteous remnant who, having taken their sins upon himself, imparts to them their righteousness as they were incorporated in him.

Having fulfilled the covenant in himself, Jesus had already begun, by the choice of twelve disciples in parallel with the twelve Old Testament tribes, to reconstitute the ancient community of Israel. The new Israel was brought about by his death, resurrection and ascension to heaven, while the apostolic community, in direct continuity with the band of disciples, was constituted by the risen Christ. Acts 2 records a specific corporate experience of tremendous power. An expectant group of disciples, met together in prayer, are lifted to a new plane of experience. The wind and the fire, symbols of power and cleansing, mark a fulfilment (as we saw in the last chapter) of the ancient prophecies concerning the universal outpouring of the Spirit. Of more abiding importance than the charismatic phenomena in themselves was the subsequent life of the apostolic church as displayed in the Book of Acts and in the New Testament Epistles. The apostolic preaching was based on the conviction that the Old Testament prophecies had been fulfilled, that Christ had inaugurated a new age, that he was born a descendant of King David, Israel's ideal ruler, that he had died according to the scriptures, that he had been buried, that he had risen again on the third day, again according to the scriptures, and was now exalted at the right hand of the Father from whose presence he would return as saviour and judge. The apostolic call was for repentance and faith, a turning away from the old life to a living belief in Christ

as saviour and Lord. Belief in him was not a notional concept but the means by which men and women were incorporated into his body as the branch was engrafted into the
vine: 'I am the true vine, and my Father is the vinegrower
... I am the vine, you are the branches. Those who abide in
me and I in them bear much fruit, because apart from me
you can do nothing' (John 15.1, 5; cf. 1 Cor. 12.12–16).
The community of those who did believe in him soon broke
the bounds of the old structures, the temple and the syna-
gogue, and saw their mission as one to the gentiles as well
as to the Jews, though the Jews remained God's unique and
ancient people whom he would not cast off (Rom. 9—11).
As God's firstborn son, Israel still bears the marks of his
gracious election, and although it is Christ who constitutes the reality and substance of God's self-revelation, it is
Christ in Israel and not apart from Israel: 'To detach Jesus
from Israel or the incarnation from its deep roots in the
covenant partnership of God with Israel would be a fatal
mistake.'[5] The church does not displace Israel but challenges Israel, and through Israel the believing gentiles as well,
to be truly the people of God. It is this community which
forms the one people of God who await the final unfolding
of the messianic kingdom.

The Spirit in the Church

If the community of faith, reconstructed by Christ exists
among humankind as the body wherein men and women
are incorporated into him, that incorporation and its ensuing and ongoing life can only be facilitated through the
work of the Holy Spirit:

---

5 Thomas F. Torrance, *The Mediation of Christ*, 2nd edn (Edinburgh:
T & T Clark, 1992), p. 23.

For just as the body is one and has many members, and all the members of the body, though many, are one body, so it is with Christ. For in the one Spirit we were all baptized into one body – Jews or Greeks, slaves or free – and we were all made to drink of one Spirit. (1 Cor. 12.12–13)

Baptism

It is because of the objective and even material character of the church, the body of Christ – the Word became *flesh*, and not merely the body of the Spirit – that entry into its communion was made by means of a *physical* rite, baptism. One of the recurrent themes in this book has been that God reveals himself through physical, material, created realities, and that the Spirit never bypasses the structures of our createdness but touches them, animates them and uses them. It is because we affirm the twin doctrines of creation and incarnation that we can have a concept of sacramentality, that is, of created, material realities being the means through which God manifests himself to us and in our world. It may well be that in an absolute sense the one true sacrament is Christ, but in a derivative sense both baptism and the Eucharist or the Lord's Supper are of vital importance for Christian faith; according to the New Testament both were instituted by Christ and each has been deemed uniquely authoritative by the church. Baptism, the sacrament of regeneration, signifies the forgiveness of sin, union with Christ in his death and resurrection, the imparting of the gift of the Spirit and being sealed with the promise of what is to come. In other words, it is through the Holy Spirit at work in baptism and affirmed by our own faith that we are born again: 'Very truly, I tell you, no one can enter the kingdom of God without being born of water and the Spirit' (John 3.5); that the sacrifice of Christ becomes effective for the washing away of our sins: 'But you were washed, you were sanctified, you were justified in the name of our Lord Jesus Christ and in the Spirit of our God' (1 Cor. 6.11); and we are identified, effectively, with Christ in his death and resurrection:

> Do you not know that all of us who have been baptized into Christ Jesus were baptized into his death? Therefore we have been buried with him by baptism into death, so that, just as Christ was raised from the dead by the glory of the Father, so we too might walk in newness of life. (Rom. 6.3–4)

It is through baptism also that we are orientated towards God's future: 'According to his mercy, through the water of rebirth and renewal by the Holy Spirit ... we might become heirs to the hope of eternal life' (Titus 5.5b–7). Baptism in no empty rite or an external ceremony but an unrepeatable sign in which individual faith and the act of God coinhere to mark the commencement of the believer's life in the Spirit: 'Those who think baptism to be inferior because "external", while the work of the Spirit is "internal", want to be wiser than God himself.'[6] To divide internal from external in this way is a false antithesis; in baptism, Spirit, water and the rite itself belong together and what God has joined together, let no one put asunder.

If what is claimed above is true, and if the weight of the New Testament evidence is in favour of baptism as a conscious choice of those who have experienced its power, why is it that since the early Christian centuries the undivided church has baptized babies? It seems that the church extended the rites and privileges of baptism beyond those who

---

6 Gerrit C. Berkouwer, *The Sacraments* (Grand Rapids: Eerdmans, 1969), p. 105.

could make a conscious response of faith for both practical and theological reasons. Practically it seemed right that family solidarity should be upheld and the children of believers as well as believers themselves should share the blessings of membership in God's family. After all, this had been the norm in Israel in the Old Testament; why should it not continue to be the norm in the reconstituted Israel of the new? Theologically infant baptism emphasized divine initiative rather than human response, an emphasis which was deemed to be doctrinally correct. 'It is a wonderful symbol of God's grace', writes William Placher, 'that, when we are too young to know what is going on and utterly powerless, we can nevertheless be made one with Christ in baptism ... It symbolizes that, before all our wanderings and errors, we were already related to God.'[7]

As it happens the author of this book belongs to a tradition that baptizes believers, not infants, whereas the majority of the book's readers were probably baptized long before they were able to understand the significance of what was done for them. This is not the place to be contentious, neither (thankfully) do we have to be! Most Christians agree on the scriptural significance of baptism, that the rite is ineffective if it does not lead to a real faith, that it should never be an occasion of 'cheap grace', a social convention which is divorced from the claims of responsible Christian nurture of membership in the church, and that water should be an essential part of the proceedings. Even if we do baptize infants and do so not by immersion but by sprinkling of water on their heads, we need to be conscious of the meaning of the sacrament in New Testament terms. Although the erstwhile secular theologian Harvey Cox

7 William C. Placher, *Jesus the Savior: The Meaning of Jesus Christ for Christian Faith* (Louisville: Westminster John Knox Press, 2001), p. 186.

speaks from within the Baptist tradition, his words sum up effectively the meaning of this sacrament for us all:

> In recent years our whole culture has begun to appreciate more and more the utter centrality of the body. We have bioenergetics, free dance, scream therapy, yoga, Tai Chi, psychodrama. Why then should baptism by immersion seem odd? In the language of the streets we talk about 'really getting into it', 'taking the plunge' 'jumping in with both feet', 'in over my head'. We believe that faith is not just a matter of ideas, not a 'head trip'. We believe it involves the whole person, or so we say. If then faith has to do with all of our life – body, mind, and spirit – with hair and belly, eyes and ankles, then we can best signify the inclusive quality of our faith by a total gesture. We don't keep a finger or a toe out. We do not use a snorkel. We allow ourselves, all of ourselves, to be plunged below the foreboding and life-giving waters. We feel it from our soles to our scalps. It tells us in a way we will never forget what faith is about.[8]

Whether we baptize babies or not, we need to be immersed in the Spirit, which the water signifies, in order to be immersed once more in the life of the world. In sacramental theology as in all else in the Christian scheme, there is no getting away from the reality of the created. However it is done, we need to be reminded constantly of the uncompromising nature of 'what faith is about'.

The Eucharist

The renewal of the life bugun once and for all, in faithful response to God's Word, in baptism occurs in the ever-

---

8 Harvey Cox, *Just As I Am* (Nashville: Abingdon Press, 1983), p. 57.

repeated though equally efficacious sign of the Eucharist or the Lord's Supper. Rooted in the Jewish Passover meal which Jesus shared with his disciples before offering himself up to death (John 13), this second physical rite became the central feature of the church's worship. Not only was this event narrated in the New Testament Gospels (Matt. 26.26–30; Mark 14.22–26; Luke 22.15–20) but it became *the* centrepiece of the apostolic tradition:

> For I received from the Lord what I also handed on to you, that the Lord Jesus on the night when he was betrayed took a loaf of bread, and when he had given thanks, he broke it and said, 'This is my body that is for you. Do this in remembrance of me.' In the same way he took the cup also, after supper, saying, 'This cup is the new covenant in my blood. Do this, as often as you drink it, in remembrance of me.' For as often as you eat this bread and drink the cup, you proclaim the Lord's death until he comes. (1 Cor. 11.23–26)

Through the great prayer of thanksgiving and the invocation of the Holy Spirit before the breaking of bread and the pouring out of the wine, the real presence of the risen Christ was confessed among his people; in the Eucharist they would remember his sacrifice, experience his presence and look forward to his coming again in glory. In a justly famous paragraph, John Macquarrie has described the exquisite richness of the Lord's Supper in a memorable way:

> The Eucharist sums up in itself Christian worship, experience and theology with amazing richness. It seems to include everything. It combines Word and Sacrament; its appeal is to spirit and to the sense; it brings together the sacrifice of Calvary and the presence of the risen Christ;

it is communion with God and communion with man; it covers the whole gamut of religious moods and emotions. Again, it teaches the doctrine of creation, as the bread, the wine and ourselves are brought to God; the doctrine of atonement, for these gifts have to be broken in order that they may be perfected; the doctrine of salvation, for the Eucharist has to do with incorporation into Christ and the sanctification of human life; above all, the doctrine of incarnation, for it is no distant God whom Christians worship but one who has made himself accessible to the world. The Eucharist also gathers up in itself the meaning of the Church; its whole action implies and sets forth our mutual interdependence in the body of Christ; it unites us with the Church of the past and even, through its paschal overtones, with the first people of God, Israel; and it points to the eschatological consummation of the kingdom of God, as an anticipation of the heavenly banquet. Comprehensive though this description is, it is likely that I have missed something out, for the Eucharist seems to be inexhaustible.[9]

Both baptism and the Eucharist contain elements of vast religious value and of theological significance for us all. They remain the twin pillars upon which the spiritual life of the Christian community are founded.

Prayer and preaching

The life of the church, however, includes more than the objective facts of the two sacraments. Among its other ordinances are prayer, preaching and the ministerial offices, all of which are aimed at effecting genuine spiritual fellow-

---

9 John Macquarrie, *Paths in Spirituality*, 2nd edn (London: SCM Press, 1992), p. 73.

ship and active discipleship in which God is glorified and humanity is served. Through prayer God is praised as the transcendent Lord, the One who creates and sustains all things; God is thanked for his bounteous goodness especially in the redemption of the world in Jesus Christ, his Son. As the holy God, rich in mercy, he is the One to whom sins must be confessed and repented of; his forgiveness, presence and guidance are invoked through the ministry of the Holy Spirit.

If God is addressed by men and women through prayer, God addresses them through the preaching of the Word. The doctrine of the Word is a dynamic affair in which God himself counsels, admonishes, leads and strengthens his people chiefly through the exposition of holy scripture. Genuine preaching should be 'a manifestation of the incarnate Word, from the written Word, by the spoken word' (Bernard Lord Manning). It is not (or should not be) a man or a woman sharing his or her personal thoughts, homespun philosophies, private experiences or innate wisdom. Such proclamation only echoes what is to be heard already in the world and reflects the very culture that the Word of God exists to challenge, judge and redeem. Genuine preaching should be rooted in scripture, open to the world and faithful to the kerygma or gospel message concerning the life, death and resurrection of Christ. It should always include a call to repentance and renewed faith. It is the preacher's task to witness to God and by so doing become the means of God's address to his people. In the words of Christoph Schwöbel: 'Behind the written word is the living word and the written word is meant to become alive again by being spoken.'[10]

---

10 Christoph Schwöbel, 'The preacher's art: preaching theologically', in Colin E. Gunton, *Theology through Preaching* (Edinburgh: T & T Clark, 2001), p. 4.

The ministry

The ministerial office, whether hierarchical as in the epis-copalian tradition of the Catholic, Anglican and Lutheran (and some Methodist) Churches, Presbyterian as practised by the United Reformed Church, the Church of Scotland and the Presbyterian Church of Wales, or egalitarian as in some Free Church traditions such as the Baptists and the Congregationalists, is pastoral in orientation and estab-lished simply 'to equip the saints for the work of ministry, for building up the body of Christ' (Eph. 4.12). The fellow-ship of the church is a fellowship in the gospel, the unity of the faithful being reconstituted by Christ in his sacrifice and resurrection, and their discipleship is such as to heed Christ's injunction about forsaking self, taking up the cross and following him:

> Then Jesus told his disciples, 'If any want to become my followers, let them deny themselves and take up their cross and follow me. For those who want to save their life will lose it, and those who lose their life for my sake will find it.' (Matt. 16.24–25)

It was Dietrich Bonhoeffer who wrote, memorably, 'When Christ calls a man, he bids him come and die.'[11] By following Christ we can no longer live for ourselves or under our own lordship; we are placed under the lordship of another and that means the death of self. Yet in exist-ing for God the church cannot but exist for the world, that which was created by God and for which Christ died. As such it is a serving community in which the enmities, divi-sions and discord of the world are striven to be overcome in

---

11 Dietrich Bonhoeffer, *The Cost of Discipleship* (London: SCM, Press 1948), p. 79; for a more recent if less arresting translation, see idem. *Discipleship: Dietrich Bonhoeffer Works* vol. 4 (Minneapolis: Fortress Press, 2001), p. 87.

the perpetual hope of Christ's coming again in glory when he will take the church up into the all-embracing and all-restoring kingdom of the Father (1 Cor. 15.22). The church is not identical with God's kingdom but it witnesses to it, points towards it and even reflects it in a partial, fragmentary and often blundering way. So despite its obvious imperfections and sometimes blatant sins, the church remains a sacrament of God's gracious presence in the world, a sign of his hope and a focus for the work of his Spirit.

The 'Marks' of the Church

It was the Council of Constantinople in AD 381 which defined the church as being 'one, holy, catholic and apostolic', and these four attributes or 'marks' have served as a basis for a Christian doctrine of the church, or ecclesiolgy, ever since.

Unity

Despite the fact that the immediate context of the Council's definition of unity was the division that had been caused by the Arian controversy, scripture itself had emphasized the fact that there was but one true God and one true community of faith. Old Testament faith had been monotheistic from its outset while the nation of Israel had been singled out by God as his particular people:

> For you are a people holy to the LORD your God; the LORD your God has chosen you out of all the peoples on earth to be his people, his treasured possession. It was not because you were more numerous than any other people that the LORD set his heart on you and chose you – for you were the fewest of all peoples. It was because the LORD loved you and kept the oath that he swore to

your ancestors, that the LORD has brought you out with a mighty hand, and redeemed you from the house of slavery, from the hand of Pharaoh king of Egypt. (Deut. 7.6–8)

In the New Testament Christ had prayed that his disciples should be one: 'I ask not only on behalf of those who will believe in me through their word, that they may all be one ... I in them and you in me, that they may become completely one' (John 17.21–23a), while the same unity in God as Father, Son and Spirit had been essential for the apostle Paul's understanding of the church (Eph. 2—3). The unity of the church does not entail directly the unity of her members but the unity of the one God in whom the three persons of Father, Son and Spirit coinhere. And just as there is but one God whose substance is shared by Father, Son and Holy Spirit, so the Father too is one, there is but one Son as there is but one Holy Spirit. It is because the church is a divine society and not merely a human construct that it must be one, its unity reflecting the divine character.

Having been called by the one God, constituted through the one Christ and sanctified in the one Spirit, membership is by way of the one baptism while the Eucharist itself reinforces this single unity:

There is one body and one Spirit, just as you were called to the one hope of your calling, one Lord, one faith, one baptism, and God and Father of all, who is above all and through all and in all. (Eph. 4.4–6)

The cup of blessing that we bless, is it not a sharing in the blood of Christ? The bread that we break, is it not a sharing in the body of Christ? Because there is one bread, we who are many are one body, for we all partake of the one bread. (1 Cor. 10.16–17)

Those who have been made members of the church by undergoing its one baptism and who have thereafter partaken of the one bread are charged with making good that unity into which they have been initiated. All Christians within the fellowship of the church are bound to live by the rule of mutual acceptance and of maintaining the unity of the Spirit through the bond of peace: 'Welcome one another, therefore, just as Christ has welcomed you, for the glory of God' (Rom. 15.7; Eph. 4.3). This unity does not mean strict uniformity in doctrine, experience or morals; how could it, if it reflects the rich variation, indeed the dazzling pluriformity, which is everywhere present within God's good creation? What it *does* imply is that there is an underlying unity among Christians which derives from their common faith in the one God and which requires them to accept one another in love: 'Put away from you all bitterness and wrath and anger and wrangling and slander, together with all malice, and be kind to one another, tenderhearted, forgiving one another, as God in Christ has forgiven you' (Eph. 4.31–32). The multiplicity of sects and denominations which have proliferated especially since the breakup of the Christian consensus of society, and seem to be destined to be part of twenty-first-century Christianity as well, must not be allowed to obscure the scriptural conviction that there is but one church witnessing to the saving reality of the one Lord who is creator, sustainer and redeemer of his one world. The church, rather, is commanded to be one 'so that the world may believe' (John 17.21).

Holiness

Holiness, in biblical parlance, refers to that which has been put aside, chosen by God and set apart for his use. As God is supremely holy, the One who is different from God's creation as its creator and Lord, so the church, having been called by God in the Old Testament and justified by Christ and sanctified by the Holy Spirit in the New Testament, is similarly holy. This holiness is not a matter of human goodness and only in a derivatory fashion a matter of morals, rather it is the fruit of God's objective calling through the gospel in which sinful and imperfect people are reconstructed into 'a holy nation' (1 Pet. 2.9) and a community of 'saints' (Rom. 1.7; 1 Cor. 1.2). This does not mean that the saints participate directly in the holiness or being of God, but that they have been called by that God to reflect who he is and who, through their calling, they are as well: 'For I am the LORD your God; sanctify yourselves therefore, and be holy, for I am holy' (Lev. 11.44). 'The Church is holy; but it is holy, not by virtue of some ontological participation in divine holiness, but by virtue of its calling by God, its reception of the divine benefits, and its obedience of faith.'[12]

It is because of this objective calling that the holy church is at all times and under all circumstances a *communio peccatorum* ('a community of sinners') despite being at the same time a *communio sanctorum* ('a communion of saints'). The immorality of the Corinthian church in the New Testament was quite scandalous while even a superficial perusal of the Pauline Epistles or the description of the churches in the Book of Revelation will show how imperfect, sinful and downright human even the early church was: 'It is actually reported that there is sexual immorality among you, and of a kind that is not found even among the pagans!' (1 Cor. 5.1). Let us not romanticize the purity or perfection of these New Testament saints. But saints they were, despite everything! The same is true of the church at all times and places, including our own. This is the only thing that can give us confidence and hope:

---

12 John Webster, *Holiness* (London: SCM Press, 2003), p. 57.

God sanctifies his church by calling the godless through Christ, by justifying sinners, and by accepting the lost. The communion or community of the saints – or the holy or the sanctified – is therefore always at the same time the community of sinners ... The church is therefore holy precisely at the point which it acknowledges its sins ... and trusts to justification through God.[13]

Despite the inevitable imperfections of the holy church as it exists in this concrete historical form, as long as it remains faithful to God and to the lordship of Christ in the Spirit, it will never forfeit its right to existence not will the gates of hell prevail against it (Matt. 16.18). As Dietrich Bonhoeffer wrote: 'Genuine love for the church will bear and love its impurity and imperfection too; for it is in fact this empirical church which nurtures God's holy treasure, his community.'[14]

Catholicity

In the time of the early Christian church, catholicity indicated the fact that the one, holy church of God was a universal society, confessing a single faith professed in baptism, and engaged in God's unique mission which would point towards the end times ('Remember I am with you always, to the end of the age' (Matt. 28.20b)) and extend to the very limits of the world ('you will be my witnesses in Jerusalem, in all Judea and Samaria, and to the ends of the earth' (Acts 1.8)). Catholicity meant, literally, 'general' or 'universal' as compared with particular or individual, and it soon came to be used of the church as a whole in comparison

13 Jürgen Moltmann, *The Church in the Power of the Spirit*, 2nd edn (London: SCM Press, 1991), p. 353.
14 Dietrich Bonhoeffer, *Sanctorum Communio: Dietrich Bonhoeffer, Works* vol. 1 (Minneapolis: Fortress Press, 1998), p. 222.

with separate churches or individual congregations. In the words of the second-century Christian leader, Ignatius of Antioch: 'Wherever Jesus Christ is present, we have the catholic Church.'[15] From this spatial and temporal designation of the word and following later threats of heresy and schism, it came to encompass the concept of wholeness or fullness and the idea of the church as guardian of the deposit of God's truth in its entirety. 'Its cathoicity', claims Jürgen Moltmann, 'means the church's inner wholeness, compared with the splitting off of individual elements of truth, which are then given an absolute validity of their own.'[16] Catholicity, then, must be allied to the idea of unity, that there is but one church of God which embraces the life and witness of his one people in all their diversity whoever they are. All sectarianism, partiality and incompleteness are incompatible with the church's confession of her own catholicity.

This has especial resonance in our own generation in terms of inclusivity and a welcoming attitude to all, especially the marginalized or oppressed. 'The church today needs to interpret the meaning of *catholic*', claims Daniel Migliore, 'as inclusive of all kinds of people.' We need hardly list those who feel themselves to be on the outside: the poor, the disadvantaged, the sinned against, victims of society's prejudices whether sexual or otherwise.

If particular racial groups and certain economic classes are being turned away from the church, either directly or indirectly, because they do not find their concerns and needs taken seriously, then it is necessary to become partisan for these people, as black theology, feminist

---

15 Ignatius of Antioch, *The Epistle to the Smyrneans* 8, in Andrew Louth (ed.), *Early Christian Writings* (Harmondsworth: Penguin Books, 1987), p. 103.
16 Moltmann, *The Church in the Power of the Spirit*, p. 348.

theology, and other forms of liberation theology do. When the church makes an option for the poor, it demonstrates rather than denies its catholicity.[17]

This, too, shows how the traditional 'marks' of the church are as relevant today as always.

Apostolicity

The root meaning of apostolic is to send forth, and in this context it refers to the sending of the apostolic witness of the risen Christ to fulfil the church's missionary task (Luke 24.48–9; John 14.25–30; Acts 1.6–11). As catholicity refers to the fullness or universal nature of the church's message, apostolicity describes the way in which that message has been handed down faithfully and sent abroad according to the command of the risen Christ. The church is thus 'built upon the foundation of the apostles amd prophets, with Jesus Christ himself as the cornerstone' (Eph. 2.20). The 'apostolic succession' or the faithful transmission, from generation to generation, of the gospel of Christ for which the apostles served as the custodians, is not, chiefly, an external rite vouchsafed by the imposition of episcopal hands, but a matter of loyalty to the revealed truth of New Testament faith. The laying on of episcopal hands as part of a historical continuity between the New Testament community and each new generation certainly *represents* that faithfulness and has often embodied it as well, but the biblical emphasis is on fidelity to the message rather than ministerial office as such. It has to to with the purity and spreading of the gospel and not with the status of bishops, however important bishops may be for the good order of the church. In the words of Moltmann once more: 'The

---

17 Daniel L. Migliore, *Faith Seeking Understanding: An Introduction to Christian Theology* (Grand Rapids: Eerdmans, 1991), p. 203.

apostolic succession is, in fact and in truth, the evangelical succession, the continuing and unadulterated proclamation of the gospel of the risen Christ.'[18]

Questions for Discussion

1 'Jesus preached the kingdom, and what emerged was the church' (Alfred Loisy). Do you think that the church is essential for Christian belief, or merely an optional extra?

2 Discuss the link between Israel and the church.

3 If the church is meant to be 'the Body of Christ', why is it so imperfect?

4 How important are the sacraments of baptism and the Lord's Supper for your faith? Could you do without them?

5 If the church is meant to be one, what is the justification for different sects and denominations?

6 How would you describe the church's apostolic mission in the twenty-first century?

---

18 Moltmann, *The Church in the Power of the Spirit*, p. 359.

10

The Christian Hope and the Life to Come

The Coming Kingdom

The study of the last things is called 'eschatology' from the Greek *eschaton*, the end, and the primary category of biblical eschatology is the kingdom of God, a term frequently used in the Gospels by Jesus. Its meaning has to do with God's rule or sovereignty rather than a geographical area. It is a dynamic notion: God's kingdom is God's rule at work: 'Your kingdom is an everlasting kingdom, and your dominion endures throughout all generations' (Ps. 145.13a).

The Old Testament belief was that Yahweh is sovereign over all things:

> The LORD is king, he is robed in majesty;
>   the LORD is robed, he is girded with strength.
> He has established the world; it shall never be moved;
>   your throne is established as of old;
>   you are from everlasting. (Ps. 93.1–2)

Yet this reign was constantly resisted or thwarted by powers within the creation, by enemies outside of Israel and often by rebellion and declension on the part of those who belonged, in fact, to God's covenant people. From this tension arose the idea that God would, either soon or eventually, vindicate his kingship unequivocally by establishing the 'day of the Lord'.

> In days to come
>   the mountain of the LORD's house
> shall be established as the highest of the mountains,
>   and shall be raised above the hills;
> all the nations shall stream to it. (Isa. 2.2)

> And the LORD will become king over all the earth; on that day the LORD will be one and his name one. (Zech. 14.9)

Frequently this idea was connected with the concept of the coming of the Messiah, the expected one, a Davidic king who would restore honour and glory to Israel:

> For a child has been born for us,
>   a son given to us;
> authority rests upon his shoulders;
>   and he is named
> Wonderful Counsellor, Mighty God,
>   Everlasting Father, Prince of Peace.
> His authority shall grow continually,
>   and there shall be endless peace
> for the throne of David and his kingdom.
>   He will establish and uphold it
> with justice and with righteousness
>   from this time onward and forevermore.
>   (Isa. 9.6–7; cf. Isa. 7.10–16; 11.1–5 etc.)

The hope, confidence and expectancy that was attached to this ideal was chastened, at times, by a sense of foreboding and of doom; the day of the Lord and the establishment of the kingdom would be no easy victory but would involve judgement and catastrophe, not least for the impenitent within Israel itself:

> Alas for you who desire the day of the LORD!
>> Why do you want the day of the LORD?
> Is not the day of the Lord darkness, not light?
>> (Amos 5.18; cf. Ezek. 38; Zech. 14)

Such was the awe-inducing character of 'the great and terrible day of the LORD' (Mal. 4.5). Yet beyond the element of judgement creation itself would be renewed. This hope was never an otherworldly hope, something ethereal or insubstantial, rather it had to do with the renewal of this-worldly realities, the rejuvenation of God's good creation and a sharing of the divine blessing with all people:

> For as the new heavens and the new earth,
>> which I will make,
> shall remain before me, says the LORD;
>> so shall your descendants and your name remain.
> From new moon to new moon,
>> and from sabbath to sabbath,
> all flesh shall come to worship before me,
> says the LORD. (Isa. 66.22–23)

The coming kingdom would inaugurate harmony and blessing and God's marred creation would be redeemed and made whole once more. When John the Baptist announced that 'the kingdom of heaven has come near' (Matt. 3.1), he did so in the context of the Old Testament expectation and hope; at long last the promised reign with its redemption of Israel, its sharing of the divine blessings with all humankind and its confidence in the renewal of all of creation was about to dawn.

It was Jesus of Nazareth who fulfilled this promise: 'Now after John was arrested, Jesus came to Galilee, proclaiming the good news of God, and saying, "The time is fulfilled, and the kindgom of God has come near; repent, and believe in the good news"' (Mark 1.14–15). That fulfilment in and with Christ was quite fundamental for early Christian belief. Christ, 'filled with the power of the Spirit', manifested the coming of the kingdom among the poor, the dispossessed and the needy in Galilee at the beginning of his public ministry, and consequently as well:

> 'The Spirit of the Lord is upon me,
>   because he has anointed me
>   to bring good news to the poor.
> He has sent me to proclaim release to the captives
>   and recovery of sight to the blind,
>   to let the oppressed go free,
> to proclaim the year of the Lord's favour' ...
> 'Today this scripture has been fulfilled in your hearing.'
> (Luke 4.18–19, 21)

There was nothing over-spiritualized or other-worldy about this ministry. Through the power of the Spirit Jesus of Nazareth reversed the effects of the fall and renewed that within God's creation which had been marred and spoiled. Whereas the Old Testament belief had posited this in the future, it was quite patent (to those who believed) that the power of the future was at work in the present and the blessings of the End Time were being experienced in the here and now. The coming kingdom had dawned.

Yet Jesus taught that this kingdom had both arrived and was still to arrive. Through his life, death and resurrection God's reign had been inaugurated in human history. As men and women believed in him, obeyed him and followed him, they entered into the promised kingdom, yet the kingdom was still to be fulfilled at the end of time in the consummation of all things in heavenly glory:

> 'You are those who have stood by me in my trials; and I confer on you, just as my Father has conferred on me, a kingdom, so that you may eat and drink at my table in my kingdom, and you will sit on thrones judging the twelve tribes of Israel.' (Luke 22.28–30)

In the New Testament writings, the Old Testament sense of God's sovereignty is transferred to the person of Christ who exercises the rule of God at the Father's right hand and through the Holy Spirit: 'Being therefore exalted at the right hand of God, and having received from the Father the promise of the Holy Spirit, he has poured out this that you both see and hear' (Acts 2.33). Whereas such terms as 'salvation' (Rom. 1.16) and being 'in Christ' (Rom. 8.1; Phil. 3.9) refer, on the whole, to a present state realized through faith, the kingdom itself is usually referred to in futurist terms: 'Then comes the end, when [Christ] hands over the kingdom of God to the Father, after he has destroyed every ruler and every authority and power; for he must reign until he has put all his enemies under his feet' (1 Cor. 15.24; cf. 1 Tim. 6.15; Rev. 1.56). What is more, the disciples of Jesus were taught to pray: 'Your kingdom come' (Luke 11.2b), an invocation which has orientated the Christian community towards God's ultimate goal for humankind and his creation ever since. So 'although an exhaustive and precise definition of this kingdom is impossible',[1] the sense of the New Testament points to the fact that the kindgom is both realized and expected; it is realized in human experience through the Holy Spirit who, on the basis of Christ's work, brings the life of the future age of glory into present

---

1 Gerrit C. Berkouwer, *The Return of Christ* (Grand Rapids: Eerdmans, 1972), p. 442.

reality, through faith; also it is expected in its fullness with the parousia or coming again of Jesus:

> I charge you to keep the commandment without spot or blame until the manifestation of our Lord Jesus Christ, which he will bring about at the right time – he who is the blessed and only Sovereign, the King of kings and Lord of lords. It is he alone who has immortality and dwells in unapproachable light, whom no one has ever seen or can see; to him be honour and eternal dominion. Amen. (1 Tim. 6.14–16)

The Second Advent

The concept of the parousia is at the heart of New Testament teaching concerning the hope of the people of God: 'Then they will see "the Son of Man coming in clouds" with great power and glory. Then he will send out the angels, and gather his elect from the four winds, from the ends of the earth to the ends of heaven' (Mark 13.26). Whatever terms were used – *parousia* meaning 'coming' or 'arrival' (Matt. 24.3; 1 Cor. 15.23; 1 Thess. 2.19 etc.); *apocalypsis* ('apocalypse') meaning 'unveiling' or 'revelation' (1 Cor. 1.7; 2 Thess. 1.7 etc.); or *epipheneia* ('epiphany') meaning 'manifestation' or 'appearing' (2 Thess. 2.8; 1 Tim. 6.14; Titus 2.13 etc.) – the vast amount of references to Christ's ultimate coming to fulfil the history of humankind and to restore creation to its intended glory (250 in all) indicate how central this motif was and should remain for genuine Christian belief. 'The eschatological', wrote Jürgen Moltmann in what has become a classic study of the subject, 'is not one element of Christianity, but is the medium of Christian faith as such, the key in which everything in it is set, the glow that suffuses everything here in the dawn of an expected new day.'[2] At the centre of eschatological reality is the motif of the second advent of Christ.

To make such a definite assertion does not mean that we have a licence to be dogmatic about the nature of the parousia. This climactic character to which the New Testament writers witness transcended anything that had been experienced hitherto, and if it was true then, it is true now. Jesus himself likened the coming to a flash of lightning: 'For as the lightning comes from the east and flashes as far as the west, so will be the coming of the Son of Man' (Matt. 24.27). It is quite obvious that we are in the realm of dramatic symbolism rather than cool prose. Yet the New Testament uniformly expected a glorious coming:

> Then the sign of the Son of Man will appear in heaven, and then all the tribes of the earth will mourn, and they will see 'the Son of Man coming on the clouds of heaven' with power and great glory. (Matt. 24.30)

> Look! He is coming with the clouds;
>   every eye will see him,
> even those who pierced him;
>   and on his account all the tribes
>   of the earth will wail.
> So it is to be. (Rev. 1.7)

This glorious coming would be decisive for the fate of humankind and for the whole of creation: 'Then comes the end, when [Christ] hands over the kingdom to God the Father ... so that God may be all in all' (1 Cor. 15.24, 28b); also, despite any 'signs' or portents of impending doom, this coming would be sudden and unexpected: 'Therefore you

---

2 Jürgen Moltmann, *Theology of Hope* (London: SCM Press, 1967), p. 16.

also must be ready, for the Son of Man is coming at an un-expected hour' (Matt. 24.44; cf Mark 13.32–37; 1 Thess. 5.1–6). The purpose of this glorious, decisive and unex-pected coming will be to complete the work of redemption and establish a new order in which Christ's original pur-poses for humankind and the creation will be realized, to resurrect the dead, to fulfil the function of judgement, and to vindicate God's people (1 Cor. 15.22–57; 2 Pet. 3.1–13; Rev. 12.1–11; 22.1–15 etc.).

The language used is apocalyptic, symbolic and met-aphorical; it is no less real for that. The context of this coming (for the early Christians) was a time of crisis: reli-gious apostasy (Mark 13.56; 2 Tim. 3.5), active persecution (Mark 13.9–11; 2 Thess. 2.1–12), conflict and war (Matt. 13.7), and although many Christians have been embar-rassed by such lurid terminology (and equally embarrassed by the use which fundamentalist preachers have made of it in their wild apocalyptic schemes), the symbols retain a unique forcefulness and evocative power. If literalism does the truth no justice at all, neither should we attempt to demythologize these concepts or explain them all away as being hopelessly outdated and naive. Pennar Davies wrote:

> While yearning for the ultimate – and speedy – triumph of Christ, the first-century Christians expected a time of tribulation and the temporary tyranny of Antichrist; and if only we would listen to the truth lying below the sur-face of this foreshortened symbolism, we could perhaps discern its meaning more amply than they could ... The promise of a time of tribulation seems not ill-founded.[3]

---

3 Pennar Davies in Roger Tomes (ed.), *Christian Confidence* (London: SPCK, 1970), p. 102; for this remarkable Welsh Congregational author and theologian, see D. Densil Morgan, *Pennar Davies* (Caerdydd: Gwasg Prifysgol Cymru, 2003).

Although the parousia is portrayed as an event which belongs as much to the realm of history as the creation of the world, the incarnation of the Son or the resurrection of Christ, its mysterious, elusive and ineffable nature is emphasized by the fact that its precise time is never revealed. Jesus expressly forbids his disciples to pry curiously about the coming of the end: 'It is not for you to know the times or periods that the Father has set by his own authority' (Acts 1.7). During the days of his flesh, even the eternal Son did not know these things: 'But about that day or hour no one knows, neither the angels of heaven, nor the Son, but only the Father' (Matt. 24.36). So the church's attitude to the parousia in the twenty-first century, as much as in the first, must be one of confidence, expectancy, yearning and hope. It must never degenerate into one of idle curiosity, apocalyptic frenzy (as it does in the popular 'rapture' theology of Christian fundamentalism) or a desire to create a road-plan or detailed map of the future. All we know is that Christ, the risen Lord, is the Lord of the future, the Alpha and the Omega, the one 'who is and who was and who is to come, the Almighty' (Rev. 1.8), and it is he who will come towards us from the future in all his glory and mercy in order to fulfil our hopes, aspirations and dreams. The only command that has been given to us is to be prepared: 'Beware, keep alert; for you do not know when the time will come ... And what I say to you I say to all: Keep awake' (Mark 13.33, 37).

Resurrection, Judgement and the Final Victory

Whereas many popular treatments of eschatology will conclude with 'the four last things: death, judgement, heaven and hell', a more rounded (and biblical) assessment of the theme will emphasize resurrection over death, the renewal of creation over other-worldliness, the corporate future of a redeemed humankind rather than the fate of atomized individuals, and how it all impacts on the way in which Christians live their lives here and now. As Colin Gunton has said: 'There may indeed be a "new" heaven and a new earth, but they remain heaven and earth, not some utterly timeless and spaceless realm, and they already bear graciously on this one.'[4] Just as there is a continuum between creation and redemption, there exists a continuity between who we are now in community, and what we shall be when Christ comes in victory and the kingdom is fulfilled:

> When by grace we rise above our egocentricity, we realize that there can be no salvation for us as persons apart from the transformation of the many communities and institutions to which we belong: family, society, humanity as a whole ... If our hope is in the triune God, it must necessarily be a hope not of the salvation of isolated individuals but of people in community.[5]

In New Testament parlance, resurrection (as we have seen in Chapter 7) has to do principally with the work of Christ. It is the basis, centrepoint and purpose of all Jesus did and everything he was: 'I am the resurrection and the life. Those who believe in me, even though they die, will live, and everyone who lives and believes in me will never die' (John 11.25–26). Yet for Jewish thought, resurrection had to do not with the fate of a crucified rabbi-carpenter from Nazareth in Galilee during the reign of Herod Antipas, but with God's universal promise for the End Time. It was not vouchsafed that an individual would be raised at

---

4 Colin E. Gunton, *The Christian Faith: An Introduction to Christian Doctrine* (Oxford: Blackwell, 2002), p. 158.
5 Daniel L. Migliore, *Faith Seeking Understanding: An Introduction to Christian Theology* (Grand Rapids: Eerdmans, 1991), p. 239

the end of his or her allotted span, but at the climax of history *all* would be raised and share in the gift of life. The way in which the early Christian church came to understand Christ's resurrection was as an anticipation of what God had promised his people at the end of the age. Resurrection still belonged to the culmination of history, but in Christ the end had already dawned and the promised future had already happened in the present; a piece of the End Time had already occurred in the midst of ordinary time and as such it was both an earnest (a pledge or a down-payment) and an anticipation of what was to come: 'But in fact Christ has been raised from the dead, the first fruits of those who have died' (1 Cor. 15.20). The fact that the first fruits had been gathered meant that the harvest was bound to follow; if the earnest had been given, there was a guarantee that the full payment was about to be made. In other words Christ's resurrection was not an isolated event, but what happened to Christ would now be shared with those who believed in him.

Despite our conviction that the resurrection is a real event that occurred (and will occur) within space, time and history, resurrection language is not straightforward language and it must be understood accordingly. 'It is not a straightforward matter to say what the Gospels understand by the resurrection of Jesus,' says Rowan Williams, 'but this seems to have something to do with the fact that the Christian communities of the last quarter of the first Christian century didn't find it all that straightforward either.'[6] The New Testament talks about bodily, fleshly resurrection, though this concept is never clarified. For the apostle Paul the resurrection body is a *spiritual* body (1 Cor. 15.44) though its physicality should not be minimized: 'Listen', he says, 'I tell you a mystery!' (1 Cor. 15.51). Resurrection is not the

---

6 Rowan Williams, *On Christian Theology* (Oxford: Blackwell, 2000), p. 187.

resuscitation of a corpse, and orthodox Christianity has always been very wary of a naive literalism in this matter as in many others. 'It now remains for me to give some suggestion of the manner of resurrection. I use this language', wrote John Calvin, 'because Paul, calling it "a mystery", urges us to sobriety, and restrains us from philosophizing too freely and subtly.'[7] What resurrection language does, nevertheless, is to assure us that God's future includes a future for created, bodily realities and not for anything as insubstantial as disembodied souls: 'The doctrine of the resurrection is not first of all about immortality, but about God's purpose for his creation, and especially his human creation'.[8] It never suggests an escape from embodiment to some heavenly, ethereal, celestial plane; rather that which exists in the body will be transformed: 'Christ will transform the body of our humiliation that it may be conformed to the body of our glory' (Phil. 3.21). In this matter, as in so much else that we have considered so far, a false other-worldliness is not a valid option.

Following resurrection comes judgement: 'For all of us must appear before the judgement seat of Christ, so that each may receive recompense for what has been done in the body, whether good or evil' (2 Cor. 5.10; cf. Rom. 14.10–12). Here again we must separate what scripture actually says, and means, from popular misconceptions of what the divine judgement is all about. The baroque splendour of Michelangelo's portrayal of the Last Judgement on the ceiling of the Sistine Chapel in Rome, where the reprobate are damned everlastingly and the blessed enjoy the delectabilities of eternal life, owes as much to the Augustinian concept of double predestination as to the New Testament evidence itself. For St Augustine, the great fifth-century

---

7 John Calvin, *Institutes of the Christian Religion* 3.25.8 (Philadelphia: Westminster Press, 1960), p. 1002.
8 Gunton, *The Christian Faith*, p. 152

Christian father, God's judgement took sin seriously and it implied an eternal damnation which was actual, severe and righteous: 'What true Christian', he wrote, 'does not believe in the punishment of the wicked?'[9] For Augustine, there was a balanced equivalent between the destinies of the saved and the damned based upon the righteousness of God's response to human sin and impenitence and his corresponding mercy: 'Who but a fool would think that God was unrighteous, either in inflicting penal justice on those who had earned it, or extending mercy to the unworthy?' he asked.[10] In the face of human unrighteousness God was under no compulsion to be merciful so the damnation of sinners was fully justified: 'If not a single member of the race had been redeemed,' he claimed, 'no one could justly have questioned the justice of God.'[11] For many centuries this remained the orthodox western teaching on the matter among both Catholics and Protestants alike, and if it is to be rejected, we must make sure that our reasons are sound.

Yet the Bible does talk about judgement, a final reckoning and indeed an ultimate separation between the saved and the lost. Significantly it is not the apostle Paul who emphasizes the idea of separation but Jesus Christ. The most dramatic picture of eschatological judgement in the New Testament is to be found in the parable of the sheep and the goats in the Gospel of Matthew where the criterion for judgement is not orthodoxy or even a living faith but our attitude to the poor, the dispossessed and the despised (Matt. 25.31–46). On the basis of this truth, Daniel

9 St Augustine, *The Enchiridion on Faith, Hope and Love* 8 (Chicago: Regnery Gateway, 1961), p. 7.
10 St Augustine, *The Enchiridion on Faith, Hope and Love* 98, p. 113.
11 St Augustine, *The Enchiridion on Faith, Hope and Love* 99, p. 116.

Migliore seems justified in claiming that 'the criteria [for being judged acceptable by God] are simple trust in God's grace and glad but usually quite unspectacular participation in Christ's agapic way of life that manifests itself in the service of others, and especially of the poor, the sick, and the outcast'.[12] The key critique of the dualist conception of judgement must be that it underplays the absolute nature of God's love in Christ, and that Christ himself not only administers judgement but has taken the judgement of hell, damnation and eternal separation from God upon himself on the cross. There is no doubt that 'the wrath of God is revealed from heaven against all ungodliness and wickedness of those who by their wickedness suppress the truth' (Rom. 1.18). But it is equally true that God has taken the full force of this holy wrath upon himself and dealt with it in our place. God has judged sin, and God, in Christ, has stood in the place where the judgement was meted out – on the cross – and by so doing has dealt with it once and for all. He is, in Karl Barth's pregnant phrase, 'the judge judged in our place': 'We know of only One who was abandoned in this way, and only One who was lost. This One is Jesus Christ. And he was lost (and found again) in order that none should be lost apart from him.'[13]

If this is true, the idea of judgement is in no way downplayed. There is no sentementalization of God or a weakheaded hankering to do away with the seriousness of sin or the harshness of the divine verdict: 'It is a stern, burning, destroying wrath. It is impossible', claims Barth, 'to make a single reservation or in any way to soften or diminish the severity of this event.'[14] Neither will anyone be spared

---

12 Migliore, *Faith Seeking Understanding*, p. 245.
13 Karl Barth, *Church Dogmatics* II/1 *The Doctrine of God* (Edinburgh: T & T Clark, 1957), p. 373.
14 Karl Barth, *Church Dogmatics* II/2 *The Doctrine of God* (Edinburgh: T & T Clark, 1957), p. 485.

this judgement; it will be universal, all-encompassing and fundamental: 'We will all have to pass into the burning, searching, purifying fire of the gracious judgement of the One who comes, and to pass through this fire no matter what the result may be.'[15] Yet it will result not in death but in life because its basis is the untold, undeserved and wholly unqualified love of God for humankind:

> For I am convinced that neither death, nor life, nor angels, nor rulers, nor things present, nor things to come, nor powers, nor height, nor depth, nor anything else in all creation, will be able to separate us from the love of God in Christ Jesus our Lord. (Rom. 8.38–39)

Will there be a universal salvation? Will all people, in the end, be included in God's final victory over sin and the renewal of his creation? The thrust of holy scripture is towards a reconciliation which is universal in scope, a view that is supported by both the Old Testament predictions of the renewal of God's good creation in the day of the Lord (Isa. 66; Zech. 14 etc.) and the New Testament vision of the day when *every* knee shall bow and *every* tongue shall confess that Jesus Christ is Lord in order for God to be 'all in all' (Phil. 2.10–11; 1 Cor. 15.28). For the early church, Christ was destined 'to gather up *all things* in him[self], things in heaven and on earth' (Eph. 1.10), and through him 'God was pleased to reconcile to himself *all things*, whether on earth or in heaven, by making peace through the blood of his cross' (Col. 1.20). It was this scriptural universalism which prompted the church's first great systematic biblical interpreter, the third-century Origen of Alexandria, to suggest (tentatively) the theory of *apocatastasis*, 'the restoration of all things'. 'There is a resurrection of the dead', he

15 Karl Barth, *Church Dogmatics* IV/3, *The Doctrine of Reconciliation* (Edinburgh: T & T Clark, 1959), p. 931.

wrote, 'and there is punishment, but not everlasting. For
when the body is punished, the soul is gradually purified,
and so is restored to its ancient rank.'[16] And again:

> We believe that at some time the Logos will have over-
> come the entire rational creature, and will have re-
> modelled every soul to his own perfection, when each
> individual, simply by the exercise of his freedom, will
> choose what the Logos wills, and will be in that state
> which he has chosen.[17]

It was not a view that gained universal approval, as much
for its speculative character as for its substantive content,
yet Origen's confident witness to God's expansive grace has
remained as a bracing challenge to the stern Augustinian-
ism of the orthodox tradition in the West. Above all things
Origen as well as Augustine (and all theologians worth their
salt ever since) desired to be faithful to scripture, though
both chose to emphasize different aspects of the same Holy
Writ. Even if we wish to stress the all-embracing range of
God's grace in Christ, we should not turn a hope into an
independent theory or presume on God's grace or take his
mercy for granted. The symbolism used by Jesus Christ indicates a solemn reality which should not be downplayed;
it was *he* who warned of 'Gehenna' [hell] (Mark 9.49), the
'unquenchable fire' (Mark 9.43, 48) and the 'outer darkness' (Matt. 8.12). It was he, also, who was sent into the
world *'not to condemn the world*, but in order that the
world might be saved through him' (John 3.17). If we con-
cur with Colin Gunton that '[W]e cannot rule out the pos-

---

16 Origen, *On First Principles* 2.10 in Henry Bettenson (ed.), *The Early
Christian Fathers*, 4th edn (Oxford: Oxford University Press, 1978), p.
258, translation revised.
17 Origen, *Contra Celsum* 8.72 (Cambridge: Cambridge University
Press, 1953), p. 116.

sibility that some may finally exclude themselves from the kingdom',[18] or even if we claim, more robustly, that there may be many impenitent souls who seem bound for disaster, we must remember that even Jesus refused to give an unequivocal answer to the question, 'Lord, will only a few be saved?' His comment should suffice for us all: 'Strive to enter through the narrow door' (Luke 13.23–24). This is a command to costly discipleship, not an invitation to speculate on things that are no concern of ours.

What is a concern of ours is that God's victory should triumph over all declension and adversity, that his will be done on earth as it is in heaven, and that we prepare ourselves for the redemption of the whole of creation. So with angels and archangels and all the company of heaven let us pray 'Amen. Come, Lord Jesus!' (Rev. 22.20).

Questions for Discussion

1 How would you define the kingdom of God? Is it manifested among people here and now, or is it something that belongs to the future?

2 'The eschatological is not one element of Christianity, but is the medium of Christian faith as such, the key in which everything in it is set, the glow that suffuses everything here in the dawn of an expected new day' (Jürgen Moltmann). Discuss.

3 How do you respond to talk about the second coming? Is it important for your own faith, and if so, how do you interpret it?

4 'For all of us must appear before the judgement seat of Christ.' Discuss.

---

18 Gunton, *The Christian Faith*, p. 164.

5 'A God without wrath brought men without sin into a
   kingdom without judgement through the ministrations
   of a Christ without a cross' (H. Richard Niebuhr). To
   what extent is this a fair criticism of our conventional
   Christianity?

6 Do you believe that God, in the end, will save
   everyone?

General Index

Index of Biblical References